Magnetic Leader

Dale Harbison Carnegie was an American writer and the developer of famous courses in self-development, salesmanship, corporate training, public speaking, and interpersonal skills. He is the author of the bestselling *How to Win Friends and Influence People*, *How to Stop Worrying and Start Living*, and many more self-help books.

The Magnetic Leader

How to Be a *Charismatic* and *Effective Leader*

Dale Carnegie

RUPA

Published by
Rupa Publications India Pvt. Ltd 2024
7/16, Ansari Road, Daryaganj
New Delhi 110002

Sales centres:
Bengaluru Chennai
Hyderabad Jaipur Kathmandu
Kolkata Mumbai Prayagraj

Edition copyright © Rupa Publications India Pvt. Ltd 2024

All rights reserved.
No part of this publication may be reproduced, transmitted, or stored in a retrieval system, in any form or by any means, electronic, mechanical, photocopying, recording or otherwise, without the prior permission of the publisher.

P-ISBN: 978-93-5702-712-0
E-ISBN: 978-93-5702-859-2

Second impression 2024

10 9 8 7 6 5 4 3 2

Printed in India

This book is sold subject to the condition that it shall not, by way of trade or otherwise, be lent, resold, hired out, or otherwise circulated, without the publisher's prior consent, in any form of binding or cover other than that in which it is published.

CONTENTS

1. Starting to Communicate — 7
2. How to Make People Like You Instantly — 21
3. The Secret of Socrates — 34
4. Thought and Reserve Power — 40
5. Make a Good First Impression — 53
6. The Short Talk to Get Attention — 62
7. Become a Good Conversationalist — 79
8. Platform Presence and Personality — 87
9. Self-Confidence Through Preparation — 106
10. Voice Charm — 125
11. Expressing Genuine Interest in Others — 130
12. How to Criticize—and Not Be Hated for It — 134
13. Making People Glad to Do What You Want — 139
14. The Talk to Convince — 145
15. No One Likes to Take Orders — 153
16. Capturing Your Audience at Once — 156

1

STARTING TO COMMUNICATE

Nothing could be easier than failing to communicate. Condescending, contradicting, berating, demeaning, treating other people as if "I am the boss, and you just work here"—until recently these were widely accepted forms of human interaction inside some of the largest and best-known companies in the world. "Barking rights" were thought to be a natural prerogative of executive positions, along with an office window and a two-hour lunch. Families, schools, and other organizations unfortunately followed suit.

For years loudness was equated with toughness. Stubbornness was equated with superior knowledge. Argumentativeness was equated with honesty. We should all—supervisor and employee, parent and child, teacher and student—be grateful those days are finally coming to an end.

Jerry Greenwald, former vice chairman of Chrysler Corporation, compares the old corporate method of communication to a trickle-down version of that childhood game, telephone. "If two teenagers live next to each other and they have something to sort out between them, one crosses the lawn, and they talk it out. If they were two people in two departments of a corporation, the teenager would tell his older brother, who would tell his mother, who would tell his father, who would go next door and tell the father of the other teenager, who would tell the other teenager's mother, and finally the other teenager would get the message and say, 'What was the guy next door trying to tell me?'

"We're trying to break all that down at Chrysler," Greenwald explained while he was still at the auto company. "If you are an operator in a plant and you need to tell someone three hundred feet at the other end of the plant to change something so you can do your job better, go over and tell him. Don't tell your foreman to tell your superintendent to tell his superintendent so that six months from now the other person will still be trying to figure out what you wanted to change."

More and more people, in businesses and elsewhere, are beginning to understand how important good communication really is. The ability to communicate well is what lights the fire in people. It's what turns great ideas into action. It's what makes all achievement possible.

Communicating well is not terribly complicated—not in theory, anyway. Communicating, after all, is something every one of us does every day in our personal lives. We've all been communicating since the early days of childhood. At least we think we have. But true communication, effective communication, is in fact relatively rare in the adult world.

START FROM THE BASICS

There's no secret recipe for learning to communicate well, but there are some basic concepts that can be mastered with relative ease. Here are the first steps to successful communication. Follow them and you will be on your way.

1. Make communication a top priority.

2. Be open to other people.
3. Create a receptive environment for communication.

No matter how busy you find yourself during the work day, *you absolutely must make time to communicate*. All the brilliant ideas in the world are worthless if you don't share them. Communication can be accomplished in many ways—in meetings, in face-to-face sessions with colleagues, just walking down the hall, or stopping at the water cooler, or spending half an hour in the company lunchroom. What's most important is that communicating never stop.

Robert Crandall has a big conference room down the hall from his chairman's office at AMR Corporation, the parent company of American Airlines. Every Monday he spends much of his day in there, listening and talking to people from all parts of the company. "Yesterday morning," Crandall said not long ago, "we had the senior officers and eight or ten or twelve other people from three or four levels in the company in there, and we were doing a very complicated analysis.

"We're trying to understand whether or not this hub-and-spoke system that we constructed has become economically indefensible as a consequence of the way the industry is changing. When we created this particular pattern of hubs and spokes, the world looked one way, and now it looks a different way. That's had an effect on how passengers flow across the system. It's also had an effect on pricing. The consequence is that we are not at all sure that the hub-and-spoke system remains viable. Determining that is very complicated.

"It takes an enormous amount of data. So we spent three and a half hours yesterday, in the course of which there were many different points of view expressed and a lot of talking back and forth and a good deal of intense feeling all around. Anyway, we finally sent people away with three or four supplementary assignments, and they'll come back in a couple of weeks with the additional data. Then we'll sit down and talk some more. 'Is what we are doing wrong? What can we do differently that has the probability of working?' That's how we eventually hope to find our way out of these dilemmas."

The benefits here are twofold: Crandall gets the input of knowledgeable people and they get to help create the future vision of American Airlines. That's fundamental to the development of trusting relationships.

Communication doesn't have to happen in big conference rooms. Some of the best corporate communication occurs in seemingly informal ways. Walter A. Green, the chairman of Harrison Conference Services, Inc., uses a technique he calls his "one-on-ones."

"Unfortunately," Green says, "in organizations we have structures. We have a president, vice presidents, and all these other levels. One-on-ones are a way of overcoming that. These are off-the-record conversations—usually at lunch—where I meet with anyone in the organization I care to meet with. It's a chance for me to stay in touch with what's important to them. How do they feel about the company? How do they feel about their jobs? I'd like to learn something about them as individuals. I like to become more human to them, and I like them to ask me questions about the company. All of that is easier one-on-one." As a result of these conversations, Green's vision for the company begins to grow.

Douglas Warner, the J.P. Morgan president, has brought this practice of direct communication into that old-line bank. "We literally walk around, walk through the inner floor," Warner says. "Go down and see some people. Get out of the office, go to other places instead of insisting that everybody come here."

Several times a week Warner or his top assistant has coffee with thirty or forty of Morgan's top people. "Eyeball-to-eyeball communication, direct and informal," in Warner's words. Even a bank like Morgan has discovered the usefulness of these simple chats. The same theory is applied inside the executive suite. "As part of all that, the managing directors of the firm, three hundred-odd people, would be invited to a large room every day for lunch—the ones who are in New York and the ones who are visiting from overseas. That way there's a real forum every day."

David Luther, corporate director of quality at Corning, Incorporated, describes this process at his organization: "I use the term bottom trawling, going to the bottom of the organization and asking, What's really going on? What are people worried about? What are they saying? What are they up against? What can you do to help?"

The need for effective communication doesn't stop at the office door. It extends to the home, to the school, to the church, even to the halls of science. Any place where people meet with people, communication is key.

It used to be that research scientists could spend their whole lives in the laboratory, singlemindedly searching for the truths of the natural order. But those days are gone. In today's competitive world, even scientists need to listen and talk.

"Many scientists don't know how to effectively communicate what they are doing," says Dr. Ronald M. Evans, an eminent research professor at the Salk Institute for Biological Studies. "They know what they are doing. They have a pretty good idea of why they're doing it. But they have difficulty putting that into perspective, transmitting the ideas outside the laboratory. It's a major limitation at many levels. To obtain funding, you have to convince people that you're doing something that's important."

When Lee Iacocca first went to work at the Ford Motor Company, he discovered the same limitation in many automobile designers and engineers: "I've known a lot of engineers with terrific ideas who had trouble explaining them to other people. It's always a shame when a guy with great talent can't tell the board or a committee what's in his head."

Without mastery of that very basic human skill—the ability to talk and listen to others—members of a company, a school, or a family can't thrive for long.

Things had gotten frenetic around the Levines' house. The children were getting older. That meant playdates, birthday parties, Little League games, gymnastics classes, Brownie troops, religious instruction—and more carpool trips for Harriet than anyone could count.

Stuart had a job he loved, but the travel was grueling and it kept him away from the family more than he would have liked. That left Harriet at home with Jesse and Elizabeth, who were terrific kids but were getting more independent by the day.

"Jesse and Elizabeth were watching far too much television," Harriet recalls, "and they weren't reading nearly enough. We barely had time to communicate."

Before things got really out of hand, the Levines all sat down together one night and came up with a plan. They would form a family council, they decided. Every Sunday after dinner they would gather around the kitchen table and talk in a calm way about whatever was on their minds. "The idea was to have a regular forum for family communication, every week, no matter what," Harriet explains.

The family council began dealing with issues large and small. Are the kids getting in their half hour of reading before television? Is Stuart going to be back in town for the soccer game? When is Harriet going to stop serving that same chicken dish?

At the end of the meeting the children would be given their weekly allowances. "Everyone is supposed to participate, and no one ever gets in trouble—as long as they tell the truth."

The biggest mistake managers used to make—besides thinking that all wisdom flowed from them—was failing to understand that communication absolutely has to be a two-way street. You have to share your ideas with others and listen to theirs. That's step number two: *Be open to other people—above, below, and beside.*

Publilius Syrus, the Roman playwright, recognized this fact of human nature two thousand years ago. "We are interested in others when they are interested in us," Syrus wrote.

If you can show your colleagues you are receptive to their ideas, they're more likely to be receptive to yours—and to keep you honestly informed about the things you need to know. Show that you care about the future of the organization and that you care as much about them. And don't limit those displays of concern to your coworkers. Communicate the same genuine caring to your customers and your clients too.

At Saunders Karp & Company, merchant banker Thomas A. Saunders III spends his professional life looking for growing companies to invest his clients' funds in. He's an expert at spotting business gems. Nothing impresses Saunders more than a company that really knows how to communicate with its customers.

He recently paid a visit to a wholesale jewelry company in Lafayette, Louisiana. He spent a day touring the company's facilities. But all it really took was five minutes in the telemarketing room for Saunders to recognize a first-string communications success.

"They handled their customers very efficiently on the phone, and the quality of the service was extremely high," Saunders said. "They didn't seem to make any mistakes. It was just bing, bing, bing, 'You want this?... Yes, we have that in stock... You want two of those, fine... You want three of those, fine... Yes, we have them... No, you have to back-order that... May I suggest a substitution?... Yes, well, if you look on page six hundred of our catalog, there's a mounting...' Boom. 'Thank you very much.' It was over in fifteen seconds. Unbelievable."

The average call took fifteen seconds, and the average customer went away thrilled. Who wouldn't put money in a company like that?

It's easy to become isolated from customers and colleagues, especially for those people who rise in an organization. But no matter how high you get, communication still has to run in all directions, talking and listening, up, down, and around the chain of command.

Ronald Reagan wasn't called the Great Communicator for nothing. Throughout his long political career he made it a point to listen and talk to the people he served. Even when he was president, Reagan continued to read constituent mail. He would have his White House secretaries give him a selection of letters each afternoon. At night he would take them up to his quarters and write out personal replies.

Bill Clinton has put the televised town meeting to much the same use: keeping himself informed about how people are feeling and showing people that he cares about them. Even if he doesn't have solutions for all the problems they bring up, there Clinton is, listening, connecting, articulating his own ideas.

There's nothing new about any of this. Abraham Lincoln took a similar approach more than a century ago. In those days, any citizen could petition the president. Sometimes Lincoln would ask an aide to respond, but frequently he would answer the petitioners personally.

He took some criticism for that. Why bother when there was a war to be fought, a union to be saved? Because Lincoln knew that understanding public opinion was an essential part of being president, and he wanted to hear it firsthand.

Richard L. Fenstermacher, executive director of North American auto operations marketing at Ford Motor Company, is a firm believer in that. "My door's open," he's constantly telling his people. "If you're walking up the hall and you see me in there, even if you just want to say hi, stop in. If you want to bounce an idea off me, do it. Don't feel you have to go through the managers."

That kind of easy interaction doesn't happen by accident. That's where rule number three comes into play: *Create a receptive environment for communication.*

GOOD COMMUNICATION THRIVES AT A HEALTHY WORK ENVIRONMENT

It's a basic fact about communicating with people: they won't say what they think—and won't listen receptively to what you say—unless a foundation of genuine trust and shared interest has been laid. You can't be insincere. How you really feel about communication, whether you're open or not, comes through loud and clear, no matter what you say. "You know right away if somebody is approachable or if they're not," Olympic gymnast Mary Lou Retton has said. "When you get that feeling, you can read a person by nonverbal communication and body language. You know when somebody is standing in the corner and saying, 'Hey, I don't want to be talked to.'"

How can you avoid sending that message? Be open, like

people, and let them know you do. Follow Retton's advice: "Being down-to-earth and humble is extremely important. I just try to put people at ease. Everybody's the same. I think everybody is on a certain level, whether you are the CEO of a company or a salesperson. It's just a different job." That's what creating a receptive environment is all about: putting people at ease.

It used to be easier than it is today. Television announcer and former baseball great Joe Garagiola remembers how much one-on-one contact there used to be between the players and the fans: "When we used to come off the field and go to our homes after the games, we would ride the subways with the same fans who were in the stands a few hours earlier.

"It wasn't uncommon for one of the fans to say, 'Hey, Joe, why did you swing at that third strike? Why didn't you let it go?' Now there isn't the same personal connection between the fan and the players other than reading about whether or not he's signing a six- or a seven-million-dollar contract."

Ray Stata, the chairman of Analog Devices, Inc., a manufacturer of high-performance integrated circuits, learned the importance of taking a personal interest from his friend Red Auerbach, the long-time president of the Boston Celtics.

Stata recalls, "When he would talk about leadership, he often used the phrase, 'I love my people.' He considered that a real prerequisite to leadership. And they have to know it. So if you have an environment where people genuinely believe that at the end of the day they can trust in your interest and concern about their well-being, then you have created relationships that have more meaning to them." Then, and only then, will the ground be appropriately prepared for communication.

Don't expect this to happen without some work.

Several years ago Corning's David Luther was trying to

convince a union leader to embrace the quality-improvement program that the company was trying to start. Luther made his pitch, talking on and on in what he thought was a very convincing way about the importance of quality improvement. This program was going to improve life for both management and labor, Luther promised the union man. But the labor leader clearly wasn't buying a word of what Luther had to say.

Luther recalls, "He got up and he said, 'Give me a break. That's baloney. You guys, that's a scam. It's better than most of your scams, but it's a scam. All you're trying to do is get more out of the workers here.'"

They kept talking, though. "He came around a little," Luther says, "but I didn't convince him, and I came to the conclusion that I could never talk my way into his trust. I could only demonstrate that I deserved it. So I said, 'I'm going to be back next year with this, and I'm going to be back the year after that, and I'm going to be back the year after that. I'm going to keep coming back with the same stuff.'" And Luther kept coming back.

His message took several years to sink in, and first he had to show he could be trusted on some smaller issues. He had to show he was listening to their concerns as well. But in the end Luther had the patience to let the message take hold, and Corning's unions became real partners in the quality-improvement program.

One last thing to remember: *Once people do take the risk of telling you what they think, don't punish them for their openness. Do nothing—absolutely nothing—to discourage them from taking the risk of communicating again.*

"If an employee makes a suggestion that I don't agree with, then I have to be very delicate about the way in which I tell them I don't agree," says Fred J. Sievert, chief financial officer of the New York Life Insurance Company. "I want to encourage them to come back to me the next time and make another suggestion. Now, I told some of the people on my staff that I may disagree with them ninety-nine times out of a hundred, but I want them to keep coming to me with their views. That's what they get paid for. The one time out of a hundred is going to be of value, and I'm not going to view them as any weaker because I disagree with them the other times."

One in a hundred. That may not sound so impressive, but great fortunes have been made on odds less certain than that. That's why listening and sharing ideas is so important.

The truth of the matter is that communication is both a skill and an art. It's a process worth thinking about and practicing more than most people do. It sometimes involves showing personal vulnerability by putting your ideas on the line. You're sharing with others and asking them to share with you. That's not always easy. It takes work and time. Techniques have to be acquired and practiced constantly. But take heart. Practice does make perfect, or very nearly so.

Kuo Chi-Zu is the chief prosecutor in Taipei, Taiwan, and a tremendously compelling public speaker. But he wasn't always so comfortable talking in front of a group. As a rising young prosecutor, Chi-Zu was always being invited to address local organizations. He said no to the Rotary. He said no to the Lions. He said no to Junior Achievement. He was so frightened of the prospect of appearing in public—as many people are—that he turned every invitation down.

"Even if I were just attending a meeting," he remembers, "I always selected the seat at the far corner. And I almost never said a single word."

He knew this fear was slowing the progress of his career—not to mention keeping him awake at night in fits of anxiety.

He knew he had to get a grip on his communication problem.

Then one day Chi-Zu was invited to speak at his old high school, and he recognized at once that this was his opportunity. He had, after all, made great effort over the years to maintain a strong relationship with the school and with its students and graduates. If there was any audience he could trust—and that would feel open to what he had to say—this was the one.

So he agreed to appear, and he prepared himself as well as he could. He chose a subject he knew a tremendous amount about and cared deeply for: his job as a prosecutor. He built the speech around real-life examples. He didn't memorize. He didn't write out the words. He just walked up to the front of the school auditorium and spoke as if he were addressing a room full of friends, which he was.

The speech was a great success. From the podium he could see the eyes in the audience riveted on him. He could hear the people laughing at his jokes. He could feel their warmth and support, and when he was finished speaking, the students rose to their feet for a robust standing ovation.

Chi-Zu learned some valuable lessons about communication that day: how communication takes a certain openness and a trusting environment, what dividends successful communication can pay. Chi-Zu didn't stop there. He became a favorite on the Taipei lecture circuit and was quickly catapulted into the chief prosecutor's job.

He was finally learning to communicate.

COMMUNICATION IS BUILT ON TRUSTING RELATIONSHIPS.

> **POINTS TO REMEMBER**
>
> 1. Good ideas turn out to be great ideas through communication.
> 2. Communication is a two-way street between an employer and employee.
> 3. A nurturing environment is crucial for healthy communication.

2

HOW TO MAKE PEOPLE LIKE YOU INSTANTLY

I was waiting in line to register a letter in the post office at Thirty-third Street and Eighth Avenue in New York. I noticed that the clerk appeared to be bored with the job—weighing envelopes, handing out stamps, making change, issuing receipts—the same monotonous grind year after year. So I said to myself: 'I am going to try to make that clerk like me. Obviously to make him like me, I must say something nice, not about myself, but about him. So I asked myself, "What is there about him that I can honestly admire?"' That is sometimes a hard question to answer, especially with strangers; but, in this case, it happened to be easy. I instantly saw something I admired no end.

So while he was weighing my envelope, I remarked with enthusiasm: 'I wish I had your head of hair.'

He looked up, half-startled, his face beaming with smiles. "Well, it isn't as good as it used to be," he said modestly. I assured him that although it might have lost some of its pristine glory, nevertheless it was still magnificent. He was immensely pleased. We carried on a pleasant little conversation and the last thing he said to me was: "Many people have admired my hair."

I'll bet that person went to lunch that day walking on air. I'll bet he went home that night and told his wife about it. I'll bet he looked in the mirror and said: "It is a beautiful head of hair."

I told this story once in public and a man asked me afterwards: "What did you want to get out of him?"

What was I trying to get out of him!!! What was I trying to get out of him!!!

If we are so contemptibly selfish that we can't radiate a little happiness and pass on a bit of honest appreciation without trying to get something out of the other person in return—if our souls are no bigger than sour crab apples, we shall meet with the failure we so richly deserve.

Oh yes, I did want something out of that chap. I wanted something priceless. And I got it. I got the feeling that I had done something for him without his being able to do anything whatever in return for me. That is a feeling that flows and sings in your memory long after the incident is past.

There is one all-important law of human conduct. If we obey that law, we shall almost never get into trouble. In fact, that law, if obeyed, will bring us countless friends and constant happiness. But the very instant we break the law, we shall get into endless trouble. The law is this: *Always make the other person feel important.* John Dewey, as we have already noted, said that the desire to be important is the deepest urge in human nature; and William James said: "The deepest principle in human nature is the craving to be appreciated." As I have already pointed out, it is this urge that differentiates us from the animals. It is this urge that has been responsible for civilization itself.

Philosophers have been speculating on the rules of human relationships for thousands of years, and out of all that speculation, there has evolved only one important precept. It is not new. It is as old as history. Zoroaster taught it to his followers in Persia 2,500 years ago. Confucius preached it in China 24 centuries ago. Lao-tse, the founder of Taoism, taught it to his disciples in the Valley of the Han. Buddha preached it on the bank of the Holy Ganges 500 years before Christ. The sacred books of Hinduism taught it among the stony hills of Judea 19 centuries ago. Jesus summed it up in one thought—probably the most important rule in the world: "Do unto others as you would have others do unto you."

You want the approval of those with whom you come in contact. You want recognition of your true worth. You want a feeling that you are important in your little world. You don't want to listen to cheap, insincere flattery, but you do crave sincere appreciation. You want your friends and associates to be, as Charles Schwab put it, "hearty in their approbation and lavish in their praise." All of us want that.

So let's obey the Golden Rule, and give unto others what we would have others give unto us.

THE PHILOSOPHY OF APPRECIATION

How? When? Where? The answer is: All the time, everywhere.

David G. Smith of Eau Claire, Wisconsin, told one of our classes how he handled a delicate situation when he was asked to take charge of the refreshment booth at a charity concert.

"The night of the concert I arrived at the park and found two elderly ladies in a very bad humor standing next to the refreshment stand. Apparently each thought that she was in charge of this project. As I stood there pondering what to do, one of the members of the sponsoring committee appeared and handed me a cash box and thanked me for taking over the project. She introduced Rose and Jane as my helpers and then ran off.

"A great silence ensued. Realizing that the cash box was a symbol of authority (of sorts), I gave the box to Rose and explained that I might not be able to keep the money straight and that if she took care of it I would feel better. I then suggested to Jane that she show two teenagers who had been assigned to refreshments how to operate the soda machine, and asked her to be responsible for that part of the project.

"The whole evening was very enjoyable with Rose happily counting the money, Jane supervising the teenagers, and me enjoying the concert."

You don't have to wait until you are ambassador to France or chairman of the Clambake Committee of your lodge before you use this philosophy of appreciation. You can work magic with it almost every day.

If, for example, the waitress brings us mashed potatoes when we have ordered French fries, let's say, "I'm sorry to trouble you, but I prefer the French fries." She'll probably reply, "No trouble at all" and will be glad to change the potatoes, because we have shown respect for her.

Little phrases such as "I'm sorry to trouble you," "Would you be so kind as to—?" "Won't you please?" "Would you mind?" "Thank you"—little courtesies like these oil the cogs of the monotonous grind of everyday life—and incidentally, they are the hallmark of good breeding.

Let's take another illustration. Hall Caine's novels—*The Christian*, *The Deemster*, *The Manxman*, among them—were all bestsellers in the early part of this century. Millions of people read his novels, countless millions. He was the son of a blacksmith. He never had more than eight years' schooling in his life; yet when he died he was the richest literary man of his time.

The story goes like this: Hall Caine loved sonnets and ballads; so he devoured all of Dante Gabriel Rossetti's poetry. He even wrote a lecture chanting the praises of Rossetti's artistic achievement—and sent a copy to Rossetti himself. Rossetti was delighted. "Any young man who has such an exalted opinion of my ability," Rossetti probably said to himself, "must be brilliant." So Rossetti invited this blacksmith's son to come to London and act as his secretary. That was the turning point in Hall Caine's life; for, in his new position, he met the literary artists of the day. Profiting by their advice and inspired by their encouragement, he launched upon a career that emblazoned his name across the sky.

His home, Greeba Castle, on the Isle of Man, became a Mecca for tourists from the far corners of the world, and he left a multimillion dollar estate. Yet—who knows—he might have died poor and unknown had he not written an essay expressing his admiration for a famous man.

Such is the power, the stupendous power, of sincere heartfelt appreciation.

Rossetti considered himself important. That is not strange. Almost everyone considers himself important, very important.

The life of many a person could probably be changed if only someone would make him feel important. Ronald J. Rowland, who is one of the instructors of our course in California, is also a teacher of arts and crafts. He wrote to us about a student named Chris in his beginning-crafts class:

> Chris was a very quiet, shy boy lacking in self-confidence, the kind of student that often does not receive the attention he deserves. I also teach an advanced class that had grown to be somewhat of a status symbol and a privilege for a student to have earned the right to be in it.

On Wednesday, Chris was diligently working at his desk. I really felt there was a hidden fire deep inside him. I asked Chris if he would like to be in the advanced class. How I wish I could express the look in Chris's face, the emotions in that shy fourteen-year-old boy, trying to hold back his tears.

"Who me, Mr Rowland? Am I good enough?"

"Yes, Chris, you are good enough."

I had to leave at that point because tears were coming to my eyes. As Chris walked out of class that day, seemingly two inches taller, he looked at me with bright blue eyes and said in a positive voice, "Thank you, Mr Rowland."

Chris taught me a lesson I will never forget—our deep desire to feel important. To help me never forget this rule, I made a sign which reads "YOU ARE IMPORTANT." This sign hangs in the front of the classroom for all to see and to remind me that each student I face is equally important.

The unvarnished truth is that almost all the people you meet feel themselves superior to you in some way, and a sure way to their hearts is to let them realize in some subtle way that you realize their importance, and recognize it sincerely.

Remember what Emerson said: "Every man I meet is my superior in some way. In that, I learn of him."

And the pathetic part of it is that frequently those who have the least justification for a feeling of achievement bolster up their egos by a show of tumult and conceit which is truly nauseating. As Shakespeare put it: "… man, proud man/Drest in a little brief authority/… Plays such fantastic tricks before high heaven/As make the angels weep."

THE KEY IMPORTANCE OF GOOD EMPLOYEES

I am going to tell you how business people in my own courses have applied these principles with remarkable results. Let's take the case of a Connecticut attorney (because of his relatives he prefers not to have his name mentioned).

Shortly after joining the course, Mr. R— drove to Long Island with his wife to visit some of her relatives. She left him to chat with an old aunt of hers and then rushed off by herself to visit some of the younger relatives. Since he soon had to give a speech professionally on how he applied the principles of appreciation, he thought he would gain some worthwhile experience talking with the elderly lady. So he looked around the house to see what he could honestly admire.

"This house was built about 1890, wasn't it?" he inquired.

"Yes," she replied, "that is precisely the year it was built."

"It reminds me of the house I was born in," he said. "It's beautiful. Well built. Roomy. You know, they don't build houses like this anymore."

"You're right," the old lady agreed. "The young folks nowadays don't care for beautiful homes. All they want is a small apartment, and then they go gadding about in their automobiles.

"This is a dream house," she said in a voice vibrating with tender memories. "This house was built with love. My husband and I dreamed about it for years before we built it. We didn't have an architect. We planned it all ourselves."

She showed Mr. R— about the house, and he expressed his hearty admiration for the beautiful treasures she had picked up in her travels and cherished over a lifetime— paisley shawls, an old English tea set, Wedgwood china, French beds and chairs, Italian paintings and silk draperies that had once hung in a French chateau.

After showing Mr. R— through the house, she took him out to the garage. There, jacked up on blocks, was a Packard car—in mint condition.

"My husband bought that car for me shortly before he passed on," she said softly. "I have never ridden in it since his death… You appreciate nice things, and I'm going to give this car to you."

"Why, aunty," he said, "you overwhelm me. I appreciate your generosity, of course; but I couldn't possibly accept it. I'm not even a relative of yours. I have a new car, and you have many relatives that would like to have that Packard."

"Relatives!" she exclaimed. "Yes, I have relatives who are just waiting till I die so they can get that car. But they are not going to get it."

"If you don't want to give it to them, you can very easily sell it to a secondhand dealer," he told her.

"Sell it!" she cried. "Do you think I would sell this car? Do you think I could stand to see strangers riding up and down the street in that car—that car that my husband bought for me? I wouldn't dream of selling it. I'm going to give it to you. You appreciate beautiful things."

He tried to get out of accepting the car, but he couldn't without hurting her feelings.

This lady, left all alone in a big house with her paisley shawls, her French antiques and her memories, was starving for a little recognition. She had once been young and beautiful and sought after. She had once built a house warm with love and had collected things from all over Europe to make it beautiful. Now, in the isolated loneliness of old age, she craved a little human warmth, a little genuine appreciation—and no one gave it to her. And when she found it, like a spring in the desert, her gratitude couldn't adequately express itself with anything less than the gift of her cherished Packard.

Let's take another case: Donald M. McMahon, who was superintendent of Lewis and Valentine, nurserymen and landscape architects in Rye, New York, related this incident:

"Shortly after I attended the talk on 'How to Win Friends and Influence People', I was landscaping the estate of a famous attorney. The owner came out to give me a few instructions about where he wished to plant a mass of rhododendrons and azaleas.

"I said, 'Judge, you have a lovely hobby. I've been admiring your beautiful dogs. I understand you win a lot of blue ribbons every year at the show in Madison Square Garden.'

"The effect of this little expression of appreciation was striking.

"'Yes,' the judge replied, 'I do have a lot of fun with my dogs. Would you like to see my kennel?'

"He spent almost an hour showing me his dogs and the prizes they had won. He even brought out their pedigrees and explained about the bloodlines responsible for such beauty and intelligence.

"Finally, turning to me, he asked: 'Do you have any small children?'

"'Yes, I do,' I replied, 'I have a son.'

"'Well, wouldn't he like a puppy?' the judge inquired.

"'Oh, yes, he'd be tickled pink.'

"'All right, I'm going to give him one,' the judge announced.

"He started to tell me how to feed the puppy. Then he paused. 'You'll forget it if I tell you. I'll write it out.' So the judge went in the house, typed out the pedigree and feeding instructions, and gave me a puppy worth several hundred dollars and one hour and fifteen minutes of his valuable time largely because I had expressed my honest admiration for his hobby and achievements."

George Eastman, of Kodak fame, invented the transparent film that made motion pictures possible, amassed a fortune of a hundred million dollars, and made himself one of the most famous business men on earth. Yet in spite of all these tremendous accomplishments, he craved little recognitions even as you and I.

To illustrate: When Eastman was building the Eastman School of Music and also Kilbourn Hall in Rochester, James Adamson, then president of the Superior Seating Company of New York, wanted to get the order to supply the theatre chairs for these buildings. Phoning the architect, Mr. Adamson made an appointment to see Mr. Eastman in Rochester.

When Adamson arrived, the architect said: "I know you want to get this order, but I can tell you right now that you won't stand a ghost of a show if you take more than five minutes of George Eastman's time. He is a strict disciplinarian. He is very busy. So tell your story quickly and get out."

Adamson was prepared to do just that.

When he was ushered into the room he saw Mr. Eastman bending over a pile of papers at his desk. Presently, Mr. Eastman looked up, removed his glasses and walked toward the architect and Mr. Adamson, saying: "Good morning, gentlemen, what can I do for you?"

The architect introduced them, and then Mr. Adamson said: "While we've been waiting for you, Mr. Eastman, I've been admiring your office. I wouldn't mind working in a room like this myself. I'm in the interior-woodworking business, and I never saw a more beautiful office in all my life."

George Eastman replied: "You remind me of something I had almost forgotten. It is beautiful, isn't it? I enjoyed it a great deal when it was first built. But I come down here now with a lot of other things on my mind and sometimes don't even see the room for weeks at a time."

Adamson walked over and rubbed his hand across a panel. "This is English oak, isn't it? A little different texture from the Italian oak."

"Yes," Eastman replied. "Imported English oak. It was selected for me by a friend who specializes in fine woods."

Then Eastman showed him about the room, commenting on the proportions, the coloring, the hand carving and other effects he had helped to plan and execute.

While drifting about the room, admiring the woodwork, they paused before a window, and George Eastman, in his modest, soft-spoken way, pointed out some of the institutions through which he was trying to help humanity: the University of Rochester, the General Hospital, the Homeopathic Hospital, the Friendly Home, the Children's Hospital. Mr. Adamson congratulated him warmly on the idealistic way he was using his wealth to alleviate the sufferings of humanity. Presently, George Eastman unlocked a glass case and pulled out the first camera he had ever owned—an invention he had bought from an Englishman.

Adamson questioned him at length about his early struggles to get started in business, and Mr. Eastman spoke with real feeling about the poverty of his childhood, telling how his widowed mother had kept a boardinghouse while he clerked in an insurance office. The terror of poverty haunted him day and night, and he resolved to make enough money so that his mother wouldn't have to work. Mr. Adamson drew him out with further questions and listened, absorbed, while he related the story of his experiments with dry photographic plates. He told how he had worked in an office all day, and sometimes experimented all night, taking only brief naps while the chemicals were working, sometimes working and sleeping in his clothes for 72 hours at a stretch.

James Adamson had been ushered into Eastman's office at ten-fifteen and had been warned that he must not take more than five minutes; but an hour had passed, then two hours passed. And they were still talking.

Finally, George Eastman turned to Adamson and said, "The last time I was in Japan I bought some chairs, brought them home, and put them in my sun porch. But the sun peeled the paint, so I went downtown the other day and bought some paint and painted the chairs myself. Would you like to see what sort of job I can do painting chairs? All right. Come up to my home and have lunch with me and I'll show you."

After lunch, Mr. Eastman showed Adamson the chairs he had brought from Japan. They weren't worth more than a few dollars, but George Eastman, now a multimillionaire, was proud of them because he himself had painted them.

The order for the seats amounted to $90,000. Who do you suppose got the order—James Adamson or one of his competitors?

From the time of this story until Mr. Eastman's death, he and James Adamson were close friends.

Claude Marais, a restaurant owner in Rouen, France, used this principle and saved his restaurant the loss of a key employee. This woman had been in his employ for five years and was a vital link between M. Marais and his staff of twenty-one people. He was shocked to receive a registered letter from her advising him of her resignation.

M. Marais reported: "I was very surprised and, even more, disappointed, because I was under the impression that I had been fair to her and receptive to her needs. Inasmuch as she was a friend as well as an employee, I probably had taken her too much for granted and maybe was even more demanding of her than of other employees.

"I could not, of course, accept this resignation without some explanation. I took her aside and said, 'Paulette, you must understand that I cannot accept your resignation. You mean a great deal to me and to this company, and you are as important to the success of this restaurant as I am.' I repeated this in front of the entire staff, and I invited her to my home and reiterated my confidence in her with my family present.

"Paulette withdrew her resignation, and today I can rely on her as never before. I frequently reinforce this by expressing my appreciation for what she does and showing her how important she is to me and to the restaurant."

"Talk to people about themselves," said Disraeli, one of the shrewdest men who ever ruled the British Empire. "Talk to people about themselves and they will listen for hours."

POINTS TO REMEMBER

1. Always make the other person feel important.
2. Act with others how you want them to act with you.
3. Old magic words will save the day.

3

THE SECRET OF SOCRATES

In talking with people, don't begin by discussing the things on which you differ. Begin by emphasizing—and keep on emphasizing—the things on which you agree. Keep emphasizing, if possible, that you are both striving for the same end and that your only difference is one of method and not of purpose.

Get the other person saying "Yes, yes" at the outset. Keep your opponent, if possible, from saying "No".

The skillful speaker gets, at the outset, a number of "Yes" responses. This sets the psychological process of the listeners moving in the affirmative direction. It is like the movement of a billiard ball. Propel in one direction, and it takes some force to deflect it; far more force to send it back in the opposite direction.

The psychological patterns here are quite clear. When a person says "No" and really means it, he or she is doing far more than saying a word of two letters. The entire organism—glandular, nervous, muscular—gathers itself together into a condition of rejection. There is, usually in minute but sometimes in observable degree, a physical withdrawal or readiness for withdrawal. The whole neuromuscular system, in short, sets itself on guard against acceptance. When, to the contrary, a person says "Yes", none of the withdrawal activities takes place. The organism is in a forward-moving, accepting, open attitude. Hence the more "yeses" we can, at the very outset, induce, the more likely we are to succeed in capturing the attention for our ultimate proposal.

It is a very simple technique—this yes response. And yet, how much it is neglected! It often seems as if people get a sense of their own importance by antagonizing others at the outset.

Get a student to say "no" at the beginning, or a customer, child, husband or wife, and it takes the wisdom and the patience of angels to transform that bristling negative into an affirmative.

The use of this "yes, yes" technique enabled James Eberson, who was a teller in the Greenwich Savings Bank, in New York City, to secure a prospective customer who might otherwise have been lost.

"This man came in to open an account," said Mr. Eberson, "and I gave him our usual form to fill out. Some of the questions he answered willingly, but there were others he flatly refused to answer.

"Before I began the study of human relations, I would have told this prospective depositor that if he refused to give the bank this information, we should have to refuse to accept this account. I am ashamed that I have been guilty of doing that very thing in the past. Naturally, an ultimatum like that made me feel good. I had shown who was boss, that the bank's rules and regulations couldn't be flouted. But that sort of attitude certainly didn't give a feeling of welcome and importance to the man who had walked in to give us his patronage.

"I resolved this morning to use a little horse sense. I resolved not to talk about what the bank wanted but about what the customer wanted. And above all else, I was determined to get him saying 'yes, yes' from the very start. So I agreed with him.

I told him the information he refused to give was not absolutely necessary.

"'However,' I said, 'suppose you have money in this bank at your death. Wouldn't you like to have the bank transfer it to your next of kin, who is entitled to it according to law?'

"'Yes, of course,' he replied.

"'Don't you think,' I continued, 'that it would be a good idea to give us the name of your next of kin so that, in the event of your death, we could carry out your wishes without error or delay?'

"Again he said, 'Yes.'

"The young man's attitude softened and changed when he realized that we weren't asking for this information for our sake but for his sake. Before leaving the bank, this young man not only gave me complete information about himself but he opened, at my suggestion, a trust account, naming his mother as the beneficiary for his account, and he had gladly answered all the questions concerning his mother also.

"I found that by getting him to say 'yes, yes' from the outset, he forgot the issue at stake and was happy to do all the things I suggested."

Joseph Allison, a sales representative for Westinghouse Electric Company, had this story to tell: "There was a man in my territory that our company was most eager to sell to. My predecessor had called on him for ten years without selling anything. When I took over the territory, I called steadily for three years without getting an order. Finally, after thirteen years of calls and sales talk, we sold him a few motors. If these proved to be all right, an order for several hundred more would follow. Such was my expectation.

"Right? I knew they would be all right. So when I called three weeks later, I was in high spirits.

"The chief engineer greeted me with this shocking announcement: 'Allison, I can't buy the remainder of the motors from you.'

"'Why?' I asked in amazement. 'Why?'

"'Because your motors are too hot. I can't put my hand on them.'

"I knew it wouldn't do any good to argue. I had tried that sort of thing too long. So I thought of getting the 'yes, yes' response.

"'Well, now look, Mr. Smith,' I said. 'I agree with you a hundred per cent; if those motors are running too hot, you ought not to buy any more of them. You must have motors that won't run any hotter than standards set by the National Electrical Manufacturers Association. Isn't that so?'

"He agreed it was. I had gotten my first 'yes.'

"'The Electrical Manufacturers Association regulations say that a properly designed motor may have a temperature of 72 degrees Fahrenheit above room temperature. Is that correct?'

"'Yes,' he agreed. 'That's quite correct. But your motors are much hotter.'

"I didn't argue with him. I merely asked: 'How hot is the mill room?'

"'Oh,' he said, 'about 75 degrees Fahrenheit.'

"'Well,' I replied, 'if the mill room is 75 degrees and you add 72 to that, that makes a total of 147 degrees Fahrenheit. Wouldn't you scald your hand if you held it under a spigot of hot water at a temperature of 147 degrees Fahrenheit?'

"Again he had to say 'yes.'

"'Well,' I suggested, 'wouldn't it be a good idea to keep your hands off those motors?'

"'Well, I guess you're right,' he admitted. We continued to chat for a while. Then he called his secretary and lined up approximately $35,000 worth of business for the ensuing month.

"It took me years and cost me countless thousands of dollars in lost business before I finally learned that it doesn't pay to argue, that it is much more profitable and much more interesting to look at things from the other person's viewpoint and try to get that person saying 'yes, yes.'"

Eddie Snow, who sponsors our courses in Oakland, California, tells how he became a good customer of a shop because the proprietor got him to say "yes, yes". Eddie had become interested in bow hunting and had spent considerable money in purchasing equipment and supplies from a local bow store. When his brother was visiting him he wanted to rent a bow for him from this store. The sales clerk told him they didn't rent bows, so Eddie phoned another bow store. Eddie described what happened:

"A very pleasant gentleman answered the phone. His response to my question for a rental was completely different from the other place. He said he was sorry but they no longer rented bows because they couldn't afford to do so. He then asked me if I had rented before. I replied, 'Yes, several years ago.' He reminded me that I probably paid $25 to $30 for the rental. I said 'yes' again. He then asked if I was the kind of person who liked to save money. Naturally, I answered 'yes.' He went on to explain that they had bow sets with all the necessary equipment on sale for $34.95. I could buy a complete set for only $4.95 more than I could rent one. He explained that is why they had discontinued renting them. Did I think that was reasonable? My 'yes' response led to a purchase of the set, and when I picked it up I purchased several more items at this shop and have since become a regular customer.'

THE SOCRATIC METHOD

Socrates, "the gadfly of Athens", was one of the greatest philosophers the world has ever known. He did something that only a handful of men in all history have been able to do: he sharply changed the whole course of human thought; and now, 24 centuries after his death, he is honored as one of the wisest persuaders who ever influenced this wrangling world.

His method? Did he tell people they were wrong? Oh, no, not Socrates. He was far too adroit for that. His whole technique, now called the "Socratic method", was based upon getting a "yes, yes" response. He asked questions with which his opponent would have to agree. He kept on winning one admission after another until he had an armful of yeses. He kept on asking questions until finally, almost without realizing it, his opponents found themselves embracing a conclusion they would have bitterly denied a few minutes previously.

The next time we are tempted to tell someone he or she is wrong, let's remember old Socrates and ask a gentle question—a question that will get the "yes, yes" response.

The Chinese have a proverb pregnant with the age-old wisdom of the Orient: "He who treads softly goes far."

POINTS TO REMEMBER

1. If you want people to listen to you, keep on emphasizing the things you both agree on.
2. The yes-response technique.
3. Ask questions with only affirmative answers.

4

THOUGHT AND RESERVE POWER

What would happen if you should overdraw your bank account? As a rule the cheque would be protested; but if you were on friendly terms with the bank, your cheque might be honored, and you would be called upon to make good the overdraft.

Nature has no such favorites, therefore extends no credits. She is as relentless as a gasoline tank—when the gas is all used, the machine stops. It is as reckless for a speaker to risk going before an audience without having something in reserve as it is for the motorist to essay a long journey in the wilds without enough gasoline in sight.

But in what does a speaker's reserve power consist? In a well-founded reliance on his general and particular grasp of his subject; in the quality of being alert and resourceful in thought—particularly in the ability to think while on his feet; and in that self-possession which makes one the captain of all his own forces, bodily and mental.

The central theme of this chapter is the second of the elements of reserve power—Thought.

THE MENTAL STOREHOUSE

An empty mind, like an empty larder, may be a serious matter or not—all will depend on the available resources. If there is no food in the cupboard the housewife does not nervously rattle the empty dishes; she telephones the grocer. If you have no ideas, do not rattle your empty "ers" and "ahs", but get some ideas, and don't speak until you do get them.

This, however, is not being what the old New England housekeeper used to call "forehanded." The real solution of the problem of what to do with an empty head is never to let it become empty. In the artesian wells of Dakota the water rushes to the surface and leaps a score of feet above the ground. The secret of this exuberant flow is of course the great supply below, crowding to get out.

What is the use of stopping to prime a mental pump when you can fill your life with the resources for an artesian well? It is not enough to have merely enough; you must have more than enough. Then the pressure of your mass of thought and feeling will maintain your flow of speech and give you the confidence and poise that denote reserve power. To be away from home with only the exact return fare leaves a great deal to circumstances!

Reserve power is magnetic. It does not consist in giving the idea that you are holding something in reserve, but rather in the suggestion that the audience is getting the cream of your observation, reading, experience, feeling, thought. To have reserve power, therefore, you must have enough milk of material on hand to supply sufficient cream.

But how shall we get the milk? There are two ways: the one is first-hand—from the cow; the other is second-hand—from the milkman.

THE SEEING EYE

Some sage has said: "For a thousand men who can speak, there is only one who can think; for a thousand men who can think, there is only one who can see." To see and to think is to get your milk from your own cow.

When the one man in a million who can see comes along, we call him Master. Old Mr. Holbrook of Cranford, asked his guest what color ash-buds were in March; she confessed she did not know, to which the old gentleman answered: "I knew you didn't. No more did I—an old fool that I am!—till this young man comes and tells me: 'Black as ash-buds in March.' And I've lived all my life in the country. More shame for me not to know. Black; they are jet-black, madam."

"This young man" referred to by Mr. Holbrook was Tennyson.

Henry Ward Beecher said: "I do not believe that I have ever met a man on the street that I did not get from him some element for a sermon. I never see anything in nature which does not work towards that for which I give the strength of my life. The material for my sermons is all the time following me and swarming up around me."

Instead of saying only one man in a million can see, it would strike nearer the truth to say that none of us sees with perfect understanding more than a fraction of what passes before our eyes, yet this faculty of acute and accurate observation is so important that no man ambitious to lead can neglect it. The next time you are in a car, look at those who sit opposite you and see what you can discover of their habits, occupations, ideals, nationalities, environments, education, and so on. You may not see a great deal the first time, but practice will reveal astonishing results. Transmute every incident of your day into a subject for a speech or an illustration. Translate all that you see into terms of speech. When you can describe all that you have seen in definite words, you are seeing clearly. You are becoming the millionth man.

De Maupassant's description of an author should also fit the public-speaker:

> His eye is like a suction pump, absorbing everything; like a pickpocket's hand, always at work. Nothing escapes him. He is constantly collecting material, gathering-up glances, gestures, intentions, everything that goes on in his presence—the slightest look, the least act, the merest trifle.

De Maupassant was himself a millionth man, a Master.

Ruskin took a common rock-crystal and saw hidden within its stolid heart lessons which have not yet ceased to move men's lives. Beecher stood for hours before the window of a jewelry store thinking out analogies between jewels and the souls of men. Gough saw in a single drop of water enough truth wherewith to quench the thirst of five thousand souls. Thoreau sat so still in the shadowy woods that birds and insects came and opened up their secret lives to his eye. Emerson observed the soul of a man so long that at length he could say, "I cannot hear what you say, for seeing what you are." Preyer for three years studied the life of his babe and so became an authority upon the child mind. Observation! Most men are blind. There are a thousand times as many hidden truths and undiscovered facts about us today as have made discoverers famous—facts waiting for some one to "pluck out the heart of their mystery." But so long as men go about the search with eyes that see not, so long will these hidden pearls lie in their shells. Not an orator but who could more effectively point and feather his shafts were he to search nature rather than libraries. Too few can see "sermons in stones" and "books in the running brooks," because they are so used to seeing merely sermons in books and only stones in running brooks. Sir Philip Sidney had a saying, "Look in thy heart and write"; Massillon explained his astute knowledge of the human heart by saying, "I learned it by studying myself;" Byron says of John Locke that "all his knowledge of the human understanding was derived from studying his own mind." Since multiform nature is all about us, originality ought not to be so rare.

THE THINKING MIND

Thinking is doing mental arithmetic with facts. Add this fact to that and you reach a certain conclusion. Subtract this truth from another and you have a definite result. Multiply this fact by another and have a precise product. See how many times this occurrence happens in that space of time and you have reached a calculable dividend. In thought-processes you perform every known problem of arithmetic and algebra. That is why mathematics is such excellent mental gymnastics. But by the same token, thinking is work. Thinking takes energy. Thinking requires time, and patience, and broad information, and clear-headedness. Beyond a miserable little surface-scratching, few people really think at all—only one in a thousand, according to the pundit already quoted. So long as the present system of education prevails and children are taught through the ear rather than through the eye, so long as they are expected to remember thoughts of others rather than think for themselves, this proportion will continue—one man in a million will be able to see, and one in a thousand to think.

But, however thought-less a mind has been, there is promise of better things as soon as the mind detects its own lack of thought-power. The first step is to stop regarding thought as "the magic of the mind," to use Byron's expression, and see it as thought truly is—a weighing of ideas and a placing of them in relationships to each other. Ponder this definition and see if you have learned to think efficiently.

Habitual thinking is just that—a habit. Habit comes of doing a thing repeatedly. The lower habits are acquired easily, the higher ones require deeper grooves if they are to persist. So we find that the thought-habit comes only with resolute practice; yet no effort will yield richer dividends. Persist in practice, and whereas you have been able to think only an inch-deep into a subject, you will soon find that you can penetrate it a foot.

Perhaps this homely metaphor will suggest how to begin the practice of consecutive thinking, by which we mean welding a number of separate thought-links into a chain that will hold. Take one link at a time, see that each naturally belongs with the ones you link to it, and remember that a single missing link means no chain.

Thinking is the most fascinating and exhilarating of all mental exercises. Once you realize that your opinion on a subject does not represent the choice you have made between what Dr. Cerebrum has written and Professor Cerebellum has said, but is the result of your own earnestly-applied brain-energy, and you will gain a confidence in your ability to speak on that subject that nothing will be able to shake. Your thought will have given you both power and reserve power.

Someone has condensed the relation of thought to knowledge in these pungent, homely lines:

Don't give me the man who thinks he thinks,
Don't give me the man who thinks he knows,

> But give me the man who knows he thinks,
> And I have the man who knows he knows!

READING AS A STIMULUS TO THOUGHT

No matter how dry the cow, however, nor how poor our ability to milk, there is still the milkman—we can read what others have seen and felt and thought. Often, indeed, such records will kindle within us that pre-essential and vital spark, the desire to be a thinker.

The following selection is taken from one of Dr. Newell Dwight Hillis's lectures, as given in *A Man's Value to Society*. Dr. Hillis is a most fluent speaker—he never refers to notes. He has reserve power. His mind is a veritable treasure-house of facts and ideas. See how he draws from a knowledge of fifteen different general or special subjects: geology, plant life, Palestine, chemistry, Eskimos, mythology, literature, the Nile, history, law, wit, evolution, religion, biography and electricity. Surely, it needs no sage to discover that the secret of this man's reserve power is the old secret of our artesian well whose abundance surges from unseen depths.

The Uses of Books and Reading

> Each Kingsley approaches a stone as a jeweler approaches a casket to unlock the hidden gems. Geikie causes the bit of hard coal to unroll the juicy bud, the thick odorous leaves, the pungent boughs, until the bit of carbon enlarges into the beauty of a tropic forest. That little book of Grant Allens called *How Plants Grow* exhibits trees and shrubs as eating, drinking and marrying. We see certain date groves in Palestine, and other date groves in the

desert a hundred miles away, and the pollen of the one carried upon the trade winds to the branches of the other. We see the tree with its strange system of water-works, pumping the sap up through pipes and mains; we see the chemical laboratory in the branches mixing flavor for the orange in one bough, mixing the juices of the pineapple in another; we behold the tree as a mother making each infant acorn ready against the long winter, rolling it in swaths soft and warm as wool blankets, wrapping it around with garments impervious to the rain, and finally slipping the infant acorn into a sleeping bag, like those the Eskimos gave Dr. Kane.

At length we come to feel that the Greeks were not far wrong in thinking each tree had a dryad in it, animating it, protecting it against destruction, dying when the tree withered. Some Faraday shows us that each drop of water is a sheath for electric forces sufficient to charge 800,000 Leyden jars, or drive an engine from Liverpool to London. Some Sir William Thomson tells us how hydrogen gas will chew up a large iron spike as a child's molars will chew off the end of a stick of candy. Thus each new book opens up some new and hitherto unexplored realm of nature. Thus books fulfill for us the legend of the wondrous glass that showed its owner all things distant and all things hidden. Through books our world becomes as "a bud from the bower of God's beauty; the sun as a spark from the light of His wisdom; the sky as a bubble on the sea of His Power." Therefore Mrs. Browning's words, "No child can be called fatherless who has God and his mother; no youth can be called friendless who has God and the companionship of good books."

Books also advantage us in that they exhibit the unity

of progress, the solidarity of the race, and the continuity of history. Authors lead us back along the pathway of law, of liberty or religion, and set us down in front of the great man in whose brain the principle had its rise. As the discoverer leads us from the mouth of the Nile back to the headwaters of Nyanza, so books exhibit great ideas and institutions, as they move forward, ever widening and deepening, like some Nile feeding many civilizations, for all the reforms of to-day go back to some reform of yesterday. Man's art goes back to Athens and Thebes. Man's laws go back to Blackstone and Justinian. Man's reapers and plows go back to the savage scratching the ground with his forked stick, drawn by the wild bullock. The heroes of liberty march forward in a solid column. Lincoln grasps the hand of Washington. Washington received his weapons at the hands of Hampden and Cromwell. The great Puritans lock hands with Luther and Savonarola.

The unbroken procession brings us at length to Him whose Sermon on the Mount was the very charter of liberty. It puts us under a divine spell to perceive that we are all co-workers with the great men, and yet single threads in the warp and woof of civilization. And when books have related us to our own age, and related all the epochs to God, whose providence is the gulf stream of history, these teachers go on to stimulate us to new and greater achievements. Alone, man is an unlighted candle. The mind needs some book to kindle its faculties. Before Byron began to write he used to give half an hour to reading some favorite passage. The thought of some great writer never failed to kindle Byron into a creative glow, even as a match lights the kindlings upon the grate. In these burning, luminous moods Byron's mind did its best work. The true book stimulates the mind as no wine can ever quicken the blood. It is reading that brings us to our best, and rouses each faculty to its most vigorous life.

We recognize this as pure cream, and if it seems at first to have its secondary source in the friendly milkman, let us not forget that the theme is The Uses of Books and Reading. Dr. Hillis both sees and thinks.

It is fashionable just now to decry the value of reading. We read, we are told, to avoid the necessity of thinking for ourselves. Books are for the mentally lazy.

Though this is only a half-truth, the element of truth it contains is large enough to make us pause. Put yourself through a good old Presbyterian soul-searching self-examination, and if reading-from-thought-laziness is one of your sins, confess it. No one can shrive you of it—but yourself. Do penance for it by using your own brains, for it is a transgression that dwarfs the growth of thought and destroys mental freedom. At first the penance will be trying—but at the last you will be glad in it.

Reading should entertain, give information, or stimulate thought. Here, however, we are chiefly concerned with information, and stimulation of thought.

WHAT SHALL I READ FOR INFORMATION?

The ample page of knowledge, as Grey tells us, is "rich with the spoils of time," and these are ours for the price of a theatre ticket. You may command Socrates and Marcus Aurelius to sit beside you and discourse of their choicest, hear Lincoln at Gettysburg and Pericles at Athens, storm the Bastile with Hugo, and wander through Paradise with Dante. You may explore darkest Africa with Stanley, penetrate the human heart with Shakespeare, chat with Carlyle about heroes, and delve with the Apostle Paul into the mysteries of faith. The general knowledge and the inspiring ideas that men have collected through ages of toil and experiment are yours for the asking. The Sage of Chelsea was right: "The true university of these days is a collection of books."

To master a worthwhile book is to master much else besides; few of us, however, make perfect conquest of a volume without first owning it physically. To read a borrowed book may be a joy, but to assign your own book a place of its own on your own shelves—be they few or many—to love the book and feel of its worn cover, to thumb it over slowly, page by page, to pencil its margins in agreement or in protest, to smile or thrill with its remembered pungencies—no mere book borrower could ever sense all that delight.

The reader who possesses books in this double sense finds also that his books possess him, and the volumes which most firmly grip his life are likely to be those it has cost him some sacrifice to own. These lightly-come-by titles, which Mr. Fatpurse selects, perhaps by proxy, can scarcely play the guide, philosopher and friend in crucial moments as do the books—long coveted, joyously attained—that are welcomed into the lives, and not merely the libraries, of us others who are at once poorer and richer.

So it is scarcely too much to say that of all the many ways in which an owned—a mastered—book is like to a human friend, the truest ways are these: A friend is worth making sacrifices for, both to gain and to keep; and our loves go out most dearly to those into whose inmost lives we have sincerely entered.

When you have not the advantage of the test of time by which to judge books, investigate as thoroughly as possible the authority of the books you read. Much that is printed and passes current is counterfeit. "I read it in a book" is to many a sufficient warranty of truth, but not to the thinker. "What book?" asks the careful mind. "Who wrote it? What does he know about the subject and what right has he to speak on it? Who recognizes him as authority? With what other recognized authorities does he agree or disagree?" Being caught trying to pass counterfeit money, even unintentionally, is an unpleasant situation. Beware lest you circulate spurious coin.

Above all, seek reading that makes you use your own brains. Such reading must be alive with fresh points of view, packed with special knowledge, and deal with subjects of vital interest. Do not confine your reading to what you already know you will agree with. Opposition wakes one up. The other road may be the better, but you will never know it unless you "give it the once over." Do not do all your thinking and investigating in front of given Q.E.D.s; merely assembling reasons to fill in between your theorem and what you want to prove will get you nowhere. Approach each subject with an open mind and—once sure that you have thought it out thoroughly and honestly—have the courage to abide by the decision of your own thought. But don't brag about it afterward.

No book on public speaking will enable you to discourse on the tariff if you know nothing about the tariff. Knowing more about it than the other man will be your only hope for making the other man listen to you.

Take a group of men discussing a governmental policy of which someone says: "It is socialistic." That will commend the policy to Mr. A, who believes in socialism, but condemn it to Mr. B, who does not. It may be that neither had considered the policy beyond noticing that its surface-color was socialistic. The chances are, furthermore, that neither Mr. A nor Mr. B has a definite idea of what socialism really is, for as Robert Louis Stevenson says, "Man lives not by bread alone but chiefly by catch-words." If you are of this group of men, and have observed this proposed government policy, and investigated it, and thought about it, what you have to say cannot fail to command their respect and approval, for you will have shown them that you possess a grasp of your subject and—to adopt an exceedingly expressive bit of slang—then some.

POINTS TO REMEMBER

1. Learn how to make use of your reserve power.
2. Attempt to see more than what meets the eye.
3. The thought-habit comes only with resolute practice; yet no effort will yield richer dividends.

5

MAKE A GOOD FIRST IMPRESSION

At a dinner party in New York, one of the guests, a woman who had inherited money, was eager to make a pleasing impression on everyone. She had squandered a modest fortune on sables, diamonds and pearls. But she hadn't done anything whatever about her face. It radiated sourness and selfishness. She didn't realize what everyone knows: namely, that the expression one wears on one's face is far more important than the clothes one wears on one's back.

Charles Schwab told me his smile had been worth a million dollars. And he was probably understating the truth. For Schwab's personality, his charm, his ability to make people like him, were almost wholly responsible for his extraordinary success; and one of the most delightful factors in his personality was his captivating smile.

Actions speak louder than words, and a smile says, "I like you. You make me happy. I am glad to see you."

That is why dogs make such a hit. They are so glad to see us that they almost jump out of their skins. So, naturally, we are glad to see them.

A baby's smile has the same effect.

Have you ever been in a doctor's waiting room and looked around at all the glum faces waiting impatiently to be seen? Dr.

Stephen K. Sproul, a veterinarian in Raytown, Missouri, told of a typical spring day when his waiting room was full of clients waiting to have their pets inoculated. No one was talking to anyone else, and all were probably thinking of a dozen other things they would rather be doing than "wasting time" sitting in that office. He told one of our classes: There were six or seven clients waiting when a young woman came in with a nine-months-old baby and a kitten. As luck would have it, she sat down next to a gentleman who was more than a little distraught about the long wait for service. The next thing he knew, the baby just looked up at him with that great big smile that is so characteristic of babies. What did that gentleman do? Just what you and I would do, of course; he smiled back at the baby. Soon he struck up a conversation with the woman about her baby and his grandchildren, and soon the entire reception room joined in, and the boredom and tension were converted into a pleasant and enjoyable experience.'

An insincere grin? No. That doesn't fool anybody. We know it is mechanical and we resent it. I am talking about a real smile, a heartwarming smile, a smile that comes from within, the kind of smile that will bring a good price in the marketplace.

Professor James V. McConnell, a psychologist at the University of Michigan, expressed his feelings about a smile. "People who smile," he said, "tend to manage, teach and sell more effectively, and to raise happier children. There's far more information in a smile than a frown. That's why encouragement is a much more effective teaching device than punishment."

The employment manager of a large New York department store told me she would rather hire a sales clerk who hadn't finished grade school, if he or she has a pleasant smile, than to hire a doctor of philosophy with a somber face.

The effect of a smile is powerful—even when it is unseen.

Telephone companies throughout the United States have a program called "phone power" which is offered to employees who use the telephone for selling their services or products. In this program they suggest that you smile when talking on the phone. Your "smile" comes through in your voice.

Robert Cryer, manager of a computer department for a Cincinnati, Ohio, company, told how he had successfully found the right applicant for a hard-to-fill position:

"I was desperately trying to recruit a Ph.D. in computer science for my department. I finally located a young man with ideal qualification who was about to be graduated from Purdue University. After several phone conversations I learned that he had several offers from other companies, many of them larger and better known than mine. I was delighted when he accepted my offer. After he started on the job, I asked him why he had chosen us over the others. He paused for a moment and then he said: 'I think it was because managers in the other companies spoke on the phone in a cold, businesslike manner, which made me feel like just another business transaction. Your voice sounded as if you were glad to hear from me…that you really wanted me to be part of your organization.' You can be assured, I am still answering my phone with a smile."

THE MAGIC SMILE

The chairman of the board of directors of one of the largest rubber companies in the United States told me that, according to his observations, people rarely succeed at anything unless they have fun doing it. This industrial leader doesn't put much faith in the old adage that hard work alone is the magic key that will unlock the door to our desires. "I have known people," he said, "who succeeded because they had a rip-roaring good time conducting their business. Later, I saw those people change as the fun became work. The business had grown dull. They lost all joy in it, and they failed."

You must have a good time meeting people if you expect them to have a good time meeting you.

I have asked thousands of business people to smile at someone every hour of the day for a week and then come to class and talk about the results. How did it work? Let's see… Here is a letter from William B. Steinhardt, a New York stockbroker. His case isn't isolated. In fact, it is typical of hundreds of cases.

"I have been married for over eighteen years," wrote Mr. Steinhardt, "and in all that time I seldom smiled at my wife or spoke two dozen words to her from the time I got up until I was ready to leave for business. I was one of the worst grouches who ever walked down Broadway.

"When you asked me to make a talk about my experience with smiles, I thought I would try it for a week. So the next morning, while combing my hair, I looked at my glum mug in the mirror and said to myself, 'Bill, you are going to wipe the scowl off that sour puss of yours today. You are going to smile. And you are going to begin right now.' As I sat down to breakfast, I greeted my wife with a 'Good morning, my dear,' and smiled as I said it.

"You warned me that she might be surprised. Well, you underestimated her reaction. She was bewildered. She was shocked. I told her that in the future she could expect this as a regular occurrence, and I kept it up every morning.

"This changed attitude of mine brought more happiness into our home in the two months since I started than there was during the last year.

"As I leave for my office, I greet the elevator operator in

the apartment house with a 'Good morning' and a smile. I greet the doorman with a smile. I smile at the cashier in the subway booth when I ask for change. As I stand on the floor of the Stock Exchange, I smile at people who until recently never saw me smile.

"I soon found that everybody was smiling back at me. I treat those who come to me with complaints or grievances in a cheerful manner. I smile as I listen to them and I find that adjustments are accomplished much easier. I find that smiles are bringing me dollars, many dollars every day.

"I share my office with another broker. One of his clerks is a likable young chap, and I was so elated about the results I was getting that I told him recently about my new philosophy of human relations. He then confessed that when I first came to share my office with his firm he thought me a terrible grouch—and only recently changed his mind. He said I was really human when I smiled.

"I have also eliminated criticism from my system. I give appreciation and praise now instead of condemnation. I have stopped talking about what I want. I am now trying to see the other person's viewpoint. And these things have literally revolutionized my life. I am a totally different man, a happier man, a richer man, richer in friendships and happiness—the only things that matter much after all."

You don't feel like smiling? Then what? Two things. First, force yourself to smile. If you are alone, force yourself to whistle or hum a tune or sing. Act as if you were already happy, and that will tend to make you happy. Here is the way the psychologist and philosopher William James put it:

"Action seems to follow feeling, but really action and feeling go together; and by regulating the action, which is under the more direct control of the will, we can indirectly regulate the feeling, which is not.

"Thus the sovereign voluntary path to cheerfulness, if our cheerfulness be lost, is to sit up cheerfully and to act and speak as if cheerfulness were already there..."

Everybody in the world is seeking happiness—and there is one sure way to find it. That is by controlling your thoughts. Happiness doesn't depend on outward conditions. It depends on inner conditions.

It isn't what you have or who you are or where you are or what you are doing that makes you happy or unhappy. It is what you think about it. For example, two people may be in the same place, doing the same thing; both may have about an equal amount of money and prestige—and yet one may be miserable and the other happy. Why? Because of a different mental attitude. I have seen just as many happy faces among the poor peasants toiling with their primitive tools in the devastating heat of the tropics as I have seen in air-conditioned offices in New York, Chicago or Los Angeles.

"There is nothing either good or bad," said Shakespeare, "but thinking makes it so."

Abe Lincoln once remarked that "most folks are about as happy as they make up their minds to be." He was right. I saw a vivid illustration of that truth as I was walking up the stairs of the Long Island Railroad station in New York. Directly in front of me thirty or forty crippled boys on canes and crutches were struggling up the stairs. One boy had to be carried up. I was astonished at their laughter and gaiety. I spoke about it to one of the men in charge of the boys. "Oh, yes," he said, "when a boy realizes that he is going to be a cripple for life, he is shocked at first; but after he gets over the shock, he usually resigns himself to his fate and then becomes as happy as normal boys."

I felt like taking my hat off to those boys. They taught me a lesson I hope I shall never forget.

GET UP AND MAKE AN EFFORT!

Working all by oneself in a closed-off room in an office not only is lonely, but it denies one the opportunity of making friends with other employees in the company. Senora Maria Gonzalez of Guadalajara, Mexico, had such a job. She envied the shared comradeship of other people in the company as she heard their chatter and laughter. As she passed them in the hall during the first weeks of her employment, she shyly looked the other way.

After a few weeks, she said to herself, "Maria, you can't expect those women to come to you. You have to go out and meet them." The next time she walked to the water cooler, she put on her brightest smile and said, "Hi, how are you today" to each of the people she met. The effect was immediate. Smiles and hellos were returned, the hallway seemed brighter, the job friendlier. Acquaintanceships developed and some ripened into friendships. Her job and her life became more pleasant and interesting.

Peruse this bit of sage advice from the essayist and publisher Elbert Hubbard—but remember, perusing it won't do you any good unless you apply it:

> Whenever you go out-of-doors, draw the chin in, carry the crown of the head high, and fill the lungs to the utmost; drink in the sunshine; greet your friends with a smile, and put soul into every handclasp. Do not fear being misunderstood and do not waste a minute thinking about your enemies. Try to fix firmly in your mind what you would like to do; and then, without veering off

direction, you will move straight to the goal. Keep your mind on the great and splendid things you would like to do, and then, as the days go gliding away, you will find yourself unconsciously seizing upon the opportunities that are required for the fulfillment of your desire, just as the coral insect takes from the running tide the element it needs. Picture in your mind the able, earnest, useful person you desire to be, and the thought you hold is hourly transforming you into that particular individual… Thought is supreme. Preserve a right mental attitude—the attitude of courage, frankness, and good cheer. To think rightly is to create. All things come through desire and every sincere prayer is answered. We become like that on which our hearts are fixed. Carry your chin in and the crown of your head high. We are gods in the chrysalis.

The ancient Chinese were a wise lot—wise in the ways of the world; and they had a proverb that you and I ought to cut out and paste inside our hats. It goes like this: "A man without a smiling face must not open a shop."

Your smile is a messenger of your goodwill. Your smile brightens the lives of all who see it. To someone who has seen a dozen people frown, scowl or turn their faces away, your smile is like the sun breaking through the clouds. Especially when that someone is under pressure from his bosses, his customers, his teachers or parents or children, a smile can help him realize that all is not hopeless—that there is joy in the world.

Some years ago, a department store in New York City, in recognition of the pressures its sales clerks were under during the Christmas rush, presented the readers of its advertisements with the following homely philosophy:

The Value of a Smile at Christmas

It costs nothing, but creates much.

It enriches those who receive, without impoverishing those who give. It happens in a flash and the memory of it sometimes lasts forever. None are so rich they can get along without it, and none so poor but are richer for its benefits.

It creates happiness in the home, fosters goodwill in a business, and is the countersign of friends.

It is rest to the weary, daylight to the discouraged, sunshine to the sad, and nature's best antidote for trouble.

Yet it cannot be bought, begged, borrowed, or stolen, for it is something that is no earthly good to anybody till it is given away.

And if in the last-minute rush of Christmas buying some of our salespeople should be too tired to give you a smile, may we ask you to leave one of yours?

For nobody needs a smile so much as those who have none left to give!

POINTS TO REMEMBER

1. Smile, it doesn't charge you anything.
2. If you think about negative things only, you'll live a miserable life.
3. Your mental attitude determines your success.

6

THE SHORT TALK TO GET ATTENTION

A famous English bishop, during World War I, spoke to the troops at Camp Upton. They were on their way to the trenches; only a very small percentage of them had any adequate idea why they were being sent. I know; I questioned them. Yet the Lord Bishop talked to these men about "International Amity," and "Serbia's Right to a Place in the Sun." Why, half of them did not know whether Serbia was a town or a disease. He might just as well have delivered a learned disquisition on the nebular hypothesis. However, not a single trooper left the hall while he was speaking; military police were stationed at every exit to prevent their escape.

I do not wish to belittle the bishop. He was every inch a scholar, and before a body of churchmen he would probably have been powerful; but he failed with these soldiers, and he failed utterly. Why? He evidently knew neither the precise purpose of his talk nor how to accomplish it.

What do we mean by the purpose of a talk? Just this: every talk, regardless of whether the speaker realizes it or not, has one of four major goals. What are they?

1. To persuade or get action.
2. To inform.

3. To impress and convince.
4. To entertain.

Let us illustrate these by a series of concrete examples from Abraham Lincoln's speaking career.

Few people know that Lincoln once invented and patented a device for lifting stranded boats off sand bars and other obstructions. He worked in a mechanic's shop near his law office making a model of his apparatus. When friends came to his office to view the model, he took no end of pains to explain it. The main purpose of those explanations was to inform.

When he delivered his immortal oration at Gettysburg, when he gave his first and second inaugural addresses, when Henry Clay died and Lincoln delivered a eulogy on his life—on all these occasions, Lincoln's main purpose was to impress and convince.

In his talks to juries, he tried to win favorable decisions. In his political talks, he tried to win votes. His purpose, then, was action.

Two years before he was elected president, Lincoln prepared a lecture on inventions. His purpose was to entertain. At least, that should have been his goal; but he was evidently not very successful in attaining it. His career as a popular lecturer was, in fact, a distinct disappointment. In one town, not a person came to hear him.

But he succeeded notably in his other speeches, some of which have become classics of human utterance. Why? Largely because in those instances he knew his goal, and he knew how to achieve it.

Because so many speakers fail to line up their purpose with the purpose of the meeting at which they are speaking, they often flounder and come to grief.

For example: A United States congressman was once hooted and hissed and forced to leave the stage of the old New York Hippodrome, because he had—unconsciously, no doubt, but nevertheless, unwisely—chosen to make an informative talk. The crowd did not want to be instructed. They wanted to be entertained. They listened to him patiently, politely, for ten minutes, a quarter of an hour, hoping the performance would come to a rapid end. But it didn't. He rambled on and on; patience snapped; the audience would not stand for more. Someone began to cheer ironically. Others took it up. In a moment, a thousand people were whistling and shouting. The speaker, obtuse and incapable as he was of sensing the temper of his audience, had the bad taste to continue. That aroused them. A battle was on. Their impatience mounted to ire. They determined to silence him. Louder and louder grew their storm of protest. Finally, the roar of it, the anger of it, drowned his words—he could not have been heard twenty feet away. So he was forced to give up, acknowledge defeat, and retire in humiliation.

Profit by his example. Fit the purpose of your talk to the audience and the occasion. If the congressman had decided in advance whether his goal of informing the audience would fit the goal of the audience in coming to the political rally, he would not have met with disaster. Choose one of the four purposes only after you have analyzed the audience and the occasion which brings them together.

To give you guidance in the important area of speech construction, this entire chapter is devoted to the short talk to get action. Each purpose demands a different organizational pattern of treatment, each has its own stumbling blocks that must be hurdled. First, let's get down to the brass tacks of organizing our talks to get the audience to act.

THE IDEAL BLUEPRINT

Is there some method of marshaling our material so that we will have the best chance for successful follow-through on what we ask the audience to do? Or is it just a matter of hit-and-miss tactics?

I remember discussing this subject with my associates back in the thirties when my classes were beginning to catch on all over the country. Because of the size of our groups we were using a two-minute limit on the talks given by class members. This limitation did not affect the talk when the purpose of the speaker was merely to entertain or inform. But when we came to the talk to actuate, that was something else. The talk to get action just didn't get off the ground when we used the old system of introduction, body, and conclusion—the organizational pattern followed by speakers since Aristotle. Something new and different was obviously needed to provide us with a sure-fire method of obtaining results in a two-minute talk designed to get action from the listeners.

We held meetings in Chicago, Los Angeles, and New York. We appealed to all our instructors, many of them on the faculties of speech departments in some of our most respected universities. Others were men who held key posts in business administration. Some were from the rapidly expanding field of advertising and promotion. From this amalgam of background and brains, we hoped to get a new approach to speech organization, one that would be streamlined, and one that would reflect our age's need for a psychological as well as a logical method for influencing the listener to act.

We were not disappointed. From those discussions came the Magic Formula of speech construction. We began using it in our classes and we have been using it ever since. What is the Magic Formula? Simply this: Start your talk by giving us the details of your Example, an incident that graphically illustrates the main idea you wish to get across. Second, in specific clearcut terms give your Point, tell exactly what you want your audience to do; and third, give your Reason, that is, highlight the advantage or benefit to be gained by the listener when he does what you ask him to do.

This is a formula highly suited to our swift-paced way of life. Speakers can no longer afford to indulge in long, leisurely introductions. Audiences are composed of busy people who want whatever the speaker has to say in straightforward language. They are accustomed to the digested, boiled-down type of journalism that presents the facts straight from the shoulder. They are exposed to hard-driving Madison Avenue advertising that shoots the message in forceful, clear terms from signboard, television screen, magazine, and newspaper. Every word is measured and nothing is wasted. By using the Magic Formula you can be certain of gaining attention and focusing it upon the main point of your message. It cautions against indulgence in vapid opening remarks, such as: "I didn't have time to prepare this talk very well," or "When your chairman asked me to talk on this subject, I wondered why he selected me." *Audiences are not interested in apologies or excuses, real or simulated.* They want *action*. In the Magic Formula you give them action from the opening word.

The formula is ideal for short talks, because it is based upon a certain amount of suspense. The listener is caught up in the story you are relating but he is not aware of what the point of your talk is until near the end of the two- or three-minute period. In cases where demands are made upon the audience, this is almost necessary for success. No speaker who wants his audience to dig deep in their pocketbooks for a cause, no matter how worthy, will get very far by starting like this: "Ladies and gentlemen. I'm here to collect five dollars from each of you." There would be a scramble for the exits. But if the speaker describes his visit to the Children's Hospital, where he saw a particularly poignant case of need, a little child who lacked financial help for an operation in a distant hospital, and then asks for contributions, the chances of getting support from his audience would be immeasurably enhanced. It is the story, the *Example,* that prepares the way for the desired action.

Note how the incident-example is used by Leland Stowe to predispose his audience to support the United Nations' Appeal for Children:

> I pray that I'll never have to do it again. Can there be anything much worse than to put only a peanut between a child and death? I hope you'll never have to do it, and live with the memory of it afterward. If you had heard their voices and seen their eyes, on that January day in the bomb-scarred workers' district of Athens…Yet all I had left was a half-pound can of peanuts. As I struggled to open it, dozens of ragged kids held me in a vise of frantically clawing bodies. Scores of mothers, with babes in their arms, pushed and fought to get within arm's reach. They held their babies out toward me. Tiny hands of skin and bone stretched convulsively. I tried to make every peanut count.
>
> In their frenzy they nearly swept me off my feet. Nothing but hundreds of hands: begging hands, clutching hands, despairing hands; all of them pitifully little hands. One salted peanut here, and one peanut there. Six peanuts knocked from my fingers, and a savage scramble of emaciated bodies at my feet. Another peanut here,

and another peanut there. Hundreds of hands, reaching and pleading; hundreds of eyes with the light of hope flickering out. I stood there helpless, an empty blue can in my hand... Yes, I hope it will never happen to you.

The Magic Formula can be used also in writing business letters and giving instructions to fellow employees and subordinates. Mothers can use it when motivating their children, and children will find it useful when appealing to their parents for a favor or privilege. You will find it a psychological tool that can be used to get your ideas across to others every day of your life.

Even in advertising, the Magic Formula is used every day. Eveready Batteries recently ran a series of radio and television commercials built upon this Formula. In the Example step, the announcer told of someone's experience of being trapped, for instance, in an overturned car late at night. After giving the graphic details of the accident, he then called upon the victim to finish the story by telling how the beams of the flashlight, powered by Eveready Batteries, brought help in time. Then the announcer went on to the Point and Reason: "Buy Eveready Batteries and you may survive a similar emergency." These stories were all true experiences out of the Eveready Battery Company's files. I don't know how many Eveready Batteries this particular advertising series sold, but I do know that the Magic Formula is an effective method of presenting what you want an audience to do, or to avoid. Let us take up the steps, one at a time.

First: Give Your Example, an Incident from Your Life

This is the part of your talk that will take up the major portion of your time. In it you describe an experience that taught you a lesson. Psychologists say we learn in two ways: one, by the Law of Exercise, in which a series of similar incidents leads to a change of our behavioral patterns; and two, by the Law of Effect, in which a *single* event may be so startling as to cause a change in our conduct. All of us have had this type of unusual experience. We do not have to search long for these incidents because they lie close to the surface of our memories. Our conduct is guided to a large extent by these experiences. By vividly reconstructing these incidents we can make them the basis of influencing the conduct of others. We can do this because people respond to words in much the same way that they respond to real happenings. In the Example part of your talk, then, you must recreate a segment of your experience in such a way that it tends to have the same effect upon your audience as it originally had upon you. This places upon you the obligation to clarify, intensify, and dramatize your experiences in a way that will make them interesting and compelling to your listeners. Below are a number of suggestions which will help to make the Example step of your action talk clear, intense, and meaningful.

Build Your Example Upon a Single Personal Experience

The incident type of example is particularly powerful when it is based upon a single event that had a dramatic impact upon your life. It may not have taken more than a few seconds, but in that short span of time you learned an unforgettable lesson. Not long ago a man in one of our classes told of a terrifying experience when he tried to swim to shore from his overturned boat. I am sure that everyone in his audience made up his mind that, faced with a similar situation, he would follow this speaker's advice and stay with the capsized boat until help came. I remember another example of a speaker's harrowing experience involving a child and an overturned power mower. That incident was so graphically etched in my mind that I will always be on guard when children are hovering near my power mower. Many of our instructors have been so impressed by what they have heard in their classes that they have acted promptly to prevent similar accidents around their homes. One keeps a fire extinguisher handy in his kitchen, for instance, because of a talk he heard which vividly recreated a tragic fire that started from a cooking accident. Another has labeled all bottles containing poison, and has seen to it that they are out of the reach of his children. This action was prompted by a talk detailing the experience of a distraught parent when she discovered her child unconscious in the bathroom with a bottle of poison clutched in her hand.

A single personal experience that taught you a lesson you will never forget is the first requisite of a persuasive action talk. With this kind of incident you can move audiences to act—if it happened to you, your listeners reason, it can happen to them, and they had better take your advice by doing what you ask them to do.

Start Your Talk With a Detail of Your Example

One of the reasons for starting your talk with the Example step is to catch attention at once. Some speakers fail to get attention with their opening words because all too often these words consist only of repetitious remarks, clichés, or fragmentary apologies that are of no interest to the audience. "Unaccustomed as I am to public speaking," is particularly offensive, but many other commonplace methods of beginning a talk are just as weak in attention-getting value. Going into the details of how you came to choose the subject, revealing to the audience that you are not too well prepared (they will discover that fact soon enough), or announcing the topic or theme of your talk like a preacher giving the text of the sermon are all methods to avoid in the short talk to get action.

Take a tip from top-flight magazine and newspaper writers: begin right in your example and you will capture the attention of your audience immediately.

Here are some opening sentences that drew my attention like a magnet: "In 1942, I found myself on a cot in a hospital"; "Yesterday at breakfast my wife was pouring the coffee and…"; "Last July I was driving at a fast clip down Highway 42…"; "The door of my office opened and Charlie Vann, our foreman, burst in"; "I was fishing in the middle of the lake; I looked up and saw a motor boat speeding toward me."

If you start your talk with phrases that answer one of the questions, Who? When? Where? What? How? or Why?, you will be using one of the oldest communication devices in the world to get attention—the story. "Once upon a time" are the magic words that open the floodgates of a child's imagination. With this same human interest approach you can captivate the minds of your listeners with your first words.

Fill Your Example with Relevant Detail

Detail, of itself, is not interesting. A room cluttered with furniture and bric-a-brac is not attractive. A picture filled with too many unrelated details does not compel the eyes to linger upon it. In the same way, too many details—unimportant details—make conversation and public speaking a boring test of endurance. The secret is to select only those details that will serve to emphasize the point and reason of the talk. If you want to get across the idea that your listeners should have their cars checked before going on a long trip, then all the details of your Example step should be concerned with what happened to you when you failed to have your car checked before taking a trip. If you tell about how you enjoyed the scenery or where you stayed when you arrived at your destination, you will only succeed in clouding the point and dissipating attention.

But relevant detail, couched in concrete, colorful language, is the best way to recreate the incident as it happened and to picturize it for the audience. To say merely that you once had an accident because of negligence is bald, uninteresting, and hardly likely to move anyone to be more careful behind the wheel of a car. But to paint a word picture of your frightening experience, using the full range of multisensory phraseology, will etch the event upon the consciousness of the listeners. For instance, here is the way one class member developed an Example step that points up vividly the need for great caution on wintry roads:

> I was driving north on Highway 41 in Indiana one morning just before Christmas, in 1949. In the car were my wife and two children. For several hours we had been creeping along on a sheet of mirror-like ice; the slightest touch on the steering wheel sent the rear of my Ford into a sickening slide. Few drivers got out of line or attempted to pass, and the hours seemed to creep as slowly as the cars.
>
> Then we came to an open stretch where the ice was melted by the sun and I stepped on the accelerator to make up for lost time. Other cars did the same. Everybody suddenly seemed in a hurry to get to Chicago first. The children began to sing in the back seat as the tension of danger subsided.
>
> The road suddenly went uphill and into a wooded area.

As the speeding car reached the top I saw, too late, that the northern slope of the hill, still untouched by the sun's rays, was like a smooth river of ice. I had a fleeting glance of two wildly careening cars in front of us and then we went into a skid. Over the shoulder we went, hopelessly out of control, and landed in a snowbank, still upright; but the car that had been following us went into a skid, too, and crashed into the side of our car, smashing in the doors and showering us with glass.

The abundance of detail in this example made it easy for the audience to project themselves into the picture. After all, your purpose is to make your audience see what you saw, hear what you heard, feel what you felt. The only way you can possibly achieve this effect is to use an abundance of concrete details. As was pointed out earlier, the task of preparation of a talk is a task of reconstructing the answers to the questions Who? When? Where? How? And Why? You must stimulate the visual imagination of your listeners by painting word pictures.

Relive Your Experience as You Relate it

In addition to using picturesque details, the speaker should relive the experience he is describing. Here is where speaking approaches its sister field of acting. All great speakers have a sense of the dramatic, but this is not a rare quality, to be found only in the eloquent. Most children have a plentiful supply of it. Many persons of our acquaintance are gifted with a sense of timing, facial expression, mimicry, or pantomime that is a part, at least, of this priceless ability to dramatize. Most of us have some skill along these lines, and with a little effort and practice we can develop more of it.

The more action and excitement you can put into the

retelling of your incident, the more it will make an impression on your listeners. No matter how rich in detail a talk may be, it will lack punch if the speaker does not give it with all the fervor of re-creation. Are you describing a fire? Give us the feeling of excitement that ran through the crowd as the firemen battled the blaze. Are you telling us about an argument with your neighbor? Relive it; dramatize it. Are you relating your final struggles in the water as panic swept over you? Make your audience feel the desperation of those awful moments in your life. For one of the purposes of the example is to make your talk memorable. Your listener will remember your talk and what you want them to do only if the example sticks in their minds. We recall George Washington's honesty because of the cherry tree incident popularized in the Weem's biography. The New Testament is a rich storehouse of principles of ethical conduct reinforced by examples full of human interest—for instance, the story of the Good Samaritan.

In addition to making your talk more easily remembered, the incident-example makes your talk more interesting, more convincing, and easier to understand. Your experience of what life has taught you is freshly perceived by the audience: they are in a sense, predetermined to respond to what you want them to do. This brings us right to the doorstep of the second phase of the Magic Formula.

Second: State Your Point, What You Want the Audience to Do

The Example step of your talk to get action has consumed more than three-quarters of your time. Assume you are talking for two minutes. You have about twenty seconds in which to hammer home the desired action you wish the audience to take and the benefit they can expect as a result of doing what you ask. The need for detail is over. The time for forthright, direct assertion has come. It is the reverse of the newspaper technique. Instead of giving the headline first, you give the news story and then you headline it with your Point or appeal for action. This step is governed by three rules:

Make the Point Brief and Specific

Be precise in telling the audience exactly what you want them to do. People will do only what they clearly understand. It is essential to ask yourself just exactly what it is you want the audience to do now that they have been disposed to action by your example. It is a good idea to write the point out as you would a telegram, trying to reduce the number of words and to make your language as clear and explicit as possible. Don't say: "Help the patients in our local orphanage." That's too general. Say instead: "Sign up tonight to meet next Sunday to take twenty-five children on a picnic." It is important to ask for an overt action, one that can be seen, rather than mental actions, which are too vague. For instance, "Think of your grandparents now and then," is too general to be acted upon. Say instead: "Make a point of visiting your grandparents this weekend." A statement such as, "Be patriotic," should be converted into "Cast your vote next Tuesday."

Make the Point Easy for Listeners to Do

No matter what the issue is, controversial or otherwise, it is the speaker's responsibility to word his point, the request for action, in such a way that it will be easy for his listeners to understand and to do. One of the best ways to do this is to be specific. If you want your listeners to improve their ability to remember names, don't say: "Start now to improve your memory of names." That is so general it is difficult to do. Say instead; "Repeat the name of the next stranger you meet five times within five minutes after you meet him."

Speakers who give detailed action points are more apt to be successful in motivating their audiences than those who rest upon generalities. To say: "Sign the get well card in the back of the room" is far better than to urge your listeners to send a card or write a letter to a hospitalized fellow class member.

The question whether to state the point negatively or positively should be answered by looking at it from the listeners' point of view. Not all negatively phrased points are ineffective. When they epitomize an avoidance attitude they are probably more convincing to listeners than a positively stated appeal. Don't be a bulb-snatcher was an avoidance phrase employed with great effect some years ago in an advertising campaign designed to sell electric light bulbs.

State the Point with Force and Conviction

The Point is the entire theme of your talk. You should give it, therefore, with forcefulness and conviction. As a headline stands out in block letters, your request for action should be emphasized by vocal animation and directness. You are about to make your last impression on the audience. Make it in such a way that the audience feels the sincerity of your appeal for action. There should be no uncertainty or diffidence about the way you ask for the order. This persuasiveness of manner should carry over to your last words, in which you give the third step of the Magic Formula.

Third: Give the Reason or Benefit the Audience May Expect

Here again, brevity and economy are necessary. In the reason step you hold out the incentive or reward the listeners may expect if they do what you have asked in the Point.

Be Sure the Reason Is Relevant to the Example

Much has been written about motivation in public speaking. It is a vast subject and a useful one for anyone engaged in persuading others to act. In the short talk to get action, on which we are centering our attention in this chapter, all you can hope to do is highlight the benefit in a sentence or two and then sit down. It is most important, however, that you focus upon the benefit that was brought out in the Example step. If you tell of your experience in saving money by buying a used car, and urge your listeners to buy a secondhand car, you must emphasize in your reason that they, too, may enjoy the economical advantages of buying secondhand. You should not deviate from the example by giving as your reason the fact that some used cars have better styling than the latest models.

Be Sure to Stress One Reason—and One Only

Most salesmen can give a half-dozen reasons why you should buy their product, and it is quite possible that you can give several reasons to back up your Point and all of them may be relevant to the Example you used. But again it is best to choose one outstanding reason or benefit and rest your case on it Your final words to the audience should be as clear-cut as the message on an advertisement in a national magazine. If you study these ads upon which so much talent has been expended, you will develop skill in handling the point and reason of your talk.

No ad attempts to sell more than one product or one idea at a time. Very few ads in the big circulation magazines use more than one reason why you should buy. The same company may change its motivational appeal from one medium to another, from television to newspapers, for instance, but rarely will the same company make different appeals in one ad, whether vocal or visual.

If you study the ads you see in magazines and newspapers and on television and analyze their content you will be amazed at how often the Magic Formula is used to persuade people to buy. You will become aware of the ribbon of relevancy which binds the whole ad or commercial together into a unified package.

There are other ways of building up an example, for instance, by using exhibits, giving a demonstration, quoting authorities, making comparisons, and citing statistics. In this chapter, the formula has been restricted to the personal incident type of example because, in the short talk to get action, it is by far the easiest and most interesting, dramatic, and persuasive method a speaker can use.

POINTS TO REMEMBER

1. The four major goals of every talk.
2. The magic formula to help your speech reach the audience's hearts and minds.
3. Fit the purpose of your talk to the audience and the occasion.

7

BECOME A GOOD CONVERSATIONALIST

What is the secret, the mystery, of a successful business interview? Well, according to former Harvard president Charles W. Eliot, "There is no mystery about successful business intercourse. Exclusive attention to the person who is speaking to you is very important. Nothing else is so flattering as that."

Eliot himself was a past master of the art of listening. Henry James, one of America's first great novelists, recalled: "Dr. Eliot's listening was not mere silence, but a form of activity. Sitting very erect on the end of his spine with hands joined in his lap, making no movement except that he revolved his thumbs around each other faster or slower, he faced his interlocutor and seemed to be hearing with his eyes as well as his ears. He listened with his mind and attentively considered what you had to say while you said it… At the end of an interview the person who had talked to him felt that he had had his say."

Self-evident, isn't it? You don't have to study for four years in Harvard to discover that. Yet I know and you know department store owners who will rent expensive space, buy their goods economically, dress their windows appealingly, spend thousands of dollars in advertising and then hire clerks who haven't the sense to be good listeners—clerks who interrupt customers, contradict them, irritate them and all but drive them from the store.

A STRONG DOSE OF SYMPATHY

Listening is just as important in one's home life as in the world of business. Millie Esposito of Croton-on-Hudson, New York, made it her business to listen carefully when one of her children wanted to speak with her. One evening she was sitting in the kitchen with her son, Robert, and after a brief discussion of something that was on his mind, Robert said: "Mom, I know that you love me very much."

Mrs. Esposito was touched and said: "Of course I love you very much. Did you doubt it?"

Robert responded: "No, but I really know you love me because whenever I want to talk to you about something you stop whatever you are doing and listen to me."

The chronic kicker, even the most violent critic, will frequently soften and be subdued in the presence of a patient, sympathetic listener—a listener who will be silent while the irate fault-finder dilates like a king cobra and spews the poison out of his system. To illustrate: The New York Telephone Company discovered a few years ago that it had to deal with one of the most vicious customers who ever cursed a customer service representative. And he did curse. He raved. He threatened to tear the phone out by its roots. He refused to pay certain charges that he declared were false. He wrote letters to the newspapers. He filed innumerable complaints with the Public Service Commission, and he started several suits against the telephone company.

At last, one of the company's most skillful "troubleshooters" was sent to interview this stormy petrel. This "troubleshooter" listened and let the cantankerous customer enjoy himself pouring out his tirade. The telephone representative listened and said "yes" and sympathized with his grievance.

"He raved on and I listened for nearly three hours," the "troubleshooter" said as he related his experiences before one of our classes. "Then I went back and listened some more. I interviewed him four times, and before the fourth visit was over I had become a charter member of an organization he was starting. He called it the 'Telephone Subscribers Protective Association.' I am still a member of this organization, and, so far as I know, I'm the only member in the world today besides Mr.—.

"I listened and sympathized with him on every point that he had made during these interviews. He had never had a telephone representative talk with him that way before, and he became almost friendly. The point on which I went to see him was not even mentioned on the first visit, nor was it mentioned on the second or third, but upon the fourth interview, I closed the case completely, he paid all his bills in full, and for the first time in the history of his difficulties with the telephone company he voluntarily withdrew his complaints from the Public Service Commission."

Doubtless Mr. — had considered himself a holy crusader, defending the public rights against callous exploitation. But in reality, what he had really wanted was a feeling of importance. He got this feeling of importance at first by kicking and complaining. But as soon as he got his feeling of importance from a representative of the company, his imagined grievances vanished into thin air.

One morning years ago, an angry customer stormed into the office of Julian F. Detmer, founder of the Detmer Woolen

Company, which later became the world's largest distributor of woolens to the tailoring trade.

"This man owed us a small sum of money," Mr. Detmer explained to me. "The customer denied it, but we knew he was wrong. So our credit department had insisted that he pay. After getting a number of letters from our credit department, he packed his grip, made a trip to Chicago, and hurried into my office to inform me not only that he was not going to pay that bill, but that he was never going to buy another dollar's worth of goods from the Detmer Woolen Company.

"I listened patiently to all he had to say. I was tempted to interrupt, but I realized that would be bad policy. So I let him talk himself out. When he finally simmered down and got in a receptive mood, I said quietly: 'I want to thank you for coming to Chicago to tell me about this. You have done me a great favor, for if our credit department has annoyed you, it may annoy other good customers, and that would be just too bad. Believe me, I am far more eager to hear this than you are to tell it.'

"That was the last thing in the world he expected me to say. I think he was a trifle disappointed, because he had come to Chicago to tell me a thing or two, but here I was thanking him instead of scrapping with him. I assured him we would wipe the charge off the books and forget it, because he was a very careful man with only one account to look after, while our clerks had to look after thousands. Therefore, he was less likely to be wrong than we were.

"I told him that I understood exactly how he felt and that, if I were in his shoes, I should undoubtedly feel precisely as he did. Since he wasn't going to buy from us anymore, I recommended some other woolen houses.

"In the past, we had usually lunched together when he came

to Chicago, so I invited him to have lunch with me this day. He accepted reluctantly, but when we came back to the office he placed a larger order than ever before. He returned home in a softened mood and, wanting to be just as fair with us as we had been with him, looked over his bills, found one had been mislaid, and sent us a cheque with his apologies.

"Later, when his wife presented him with a baby boy, he gave his son the middle name of Detmer, and he remained a friend and customer of the house until his death twenty-two years afterwards."

TECHNIQUE TO EITHER ATTRACT OR REPEL

Years ago, a poor Dutch immigrant boy washed the windows of a bakery shop after school to help support his family. His people were so poor that in addition he used to go out in the street with a basket every day and collect stray bits of coal that had fallen in the gutter where the coal wagons had delivered fuel. That boy, Edward Bok, never got more than six years of schooling in his life; yet eventually he made himself one of the most successful magazine editors in the history of American journalism. How did he do it? That is a long story, but how he got his start can be told briefly. He got his start by using the principles in this chapter.

He left school when he was 13, and became an office boy for Western Union, but he didn't for one moment give up the idea of an education. Instead, he started to educate himself. He saved his carfares and went without lunch until he had enough money to buy an encyclopedia of American biography—and then he did an unheard-of thing. He read the lives of famous people and wrote to them asking for additional information about their childhoods. He was a good listener. He asked famous people to tell him more about themselves. He wrote to General James A. Garfield, who was then running for president, and asked if it was true that he was once a tow boy on a canal; and Garfield replied. He wrote to General Grant asking about a certain battle, and Grant drew a map for him and invited this 14-year-old boy to dinner and spent the evening talking to him.

Soon our Western Union messenger boy was corresponding with many of the most famous people in the nation: Ralph Waldo Emerson, Oliver Wendell Holmes, Longfellow, Mrs. Abraham Lincoln, Louisa May Alcott, General Sherman and Jefferson Davis. Not only did he correspond with these distinguished people, but as soon as he got a vacation, he visited many of them as a welcome guest in their homes. This experience imbued him with a confidence that was invaluable. These men and women fired him with a vision and ambition that shaped his life. And all this, let me repeat, was made possible solely by the application of the principles we are discussing here.

Isaac F. Marcosson, a journalist who interviewed hundreds of celebrities, declared that many people fail to make a favorable impression because they don't listen attentively. "They have been so much concerned with what they are going to say next that they do not keep their ears open... Very important people have told me that they prefer good listeners to good talkers, but the ability to listen seems rarer than almost any other good trait."

And not only important personages crave a good listener, but ordinary folk do too. As the *Reader's Digest* once said: "Many persons call a doctor when all they want is an audience."

During the darkest hours of the Civil War, Lincoln wrote to an old friend in Springfield, Illinois, asking him to come to Washington. Lincoln said he had some problems he wanted to discuss with him. The old neighbor called at the White House, and Lincoln talked to him for hours about the advisability of issuing a proclamation freeing the slaves. Lincoln went over all the arguments for and against such a move, and then read letters and newspaper articles, some denouncing him for not freeing the slaves and others denouncing him for fear he was going to free them. After talking for hours, Lincoln shook hands with his old neighbor, said good night, and sent him back to Illinois without even asking for his opinion. Lincoln had done all the talking himself. That seemed to clarify his mind. "He seemed to feel easier after that talk," the old friend said. Lincoln hadn't wanted advice. He had wanted merely a friendly, sympathetic listener to whom he could unburden himself. That's what we all want when we are in trouble. That is frequently all the irritated customer wants, and the dissatisfied employee or the hurt friend.

One of the great listeners of modern times was Sigmund Freud. A man who met Freud described his manner of listening. "It struck me so forcibly that I shall never forget him. He had qualities which I had never seen in any other man. Never had I seen such concentrated attention. There was none of the piercing 'soul penetrating gaze' business. His eyes were mild and genial. His voice was low and kind. His gestures were few. But the attention he gave me, his appreciation of what I said, even when I said it badly, was extraordinary. *You've no idea what it meant to be listened to like that.*"

If you want to know how to make people shun you and laugh at you behind your back and even despise you, here is the recipe: Never listen to anyone for long. Talk incessantly about yourself. If you have an idea while the other person is talking, don't wait for him or her to finish: bust right in and interrupt in the middle of a sentence.

Do you know people like that? I do, unfortunately; and

the astonishing part of it is that some of them are prominent.

Bores, that is all they are—bores intoxicated with their own egos, drunk with a sense of their own importance.

People who talk only of themselves think only of themselves. And "those people who think only of themselves," Dr. Nicholas Murray Butler, longtime president of Columbia University, said, "are hopelessly uneducated. They are not educated, no matter how instructed they may be." So if you aspire to be a good conversationalist, be an attentive listener. To be interesting, be interested. Ask questions that other persons will enjoy answering. Encourage them to talk about themselves and their accomplishments.

Remember that the people you are talking to are a hundred times more interested in themselves and their wants and problems than they are in you and your problems. A person's toothache means more to that person than a famine in China which kills a million people. A boil on one's neck interests one more than 40 earthquakes in Africa. Think of that the next time you start a conversation.

POINTS TO REMEMBER

1. A good conversationalist is a good listener first.
2. Being attentive is appreciated.
3. Encourage others to have a conversation with you by appearing interested.

8

PLATFORM PRESENCE AND PERSONALITY

The Carnegie Institute of Technology at one time gave intelligence tests to one hundred prominent businessmen. The tests were similar to those used in the army during the war, and the results led the institute to declare that personality contributes more to business success than does superior intelligence.

That is a very significant pronouncement: very significant for the businessman, very significant for the educator, very significant for the professional man, very significant for the speaker.

Personality—with the exception of preparation—is probably the most important factor in public address. "In eloquent speaking," declared Elbert Hubbard, "it is manner that wins, not words." Rather it is manner plus ideas. But personality is a vague and elusive thing, defying analysis like the perfume of the violet. It is the whole combination of the man, the physical, the spiritual, the mental; his traits, his predilections, his tendencies, his temperament, his cast of mind, his vigor, his experience, his training, his life. It is as complex as Einstein's theory of relativity, almost as little understood.

A man's personality is very largely the result of his inheritances. It is largely determined before birth. True, his later environment has something to do with it. But, all in all, it is an extremely difficult factor to alter or improve. Yet we can, by taking thought, strengthen it to some extent and make it more forceful, more attractive. At any rate, we can strive to get the utmost possible out of this strange thing that nature has given us. The subject is of vast importance to every one of us. The possibilities for improvement, limited as they are, are still large enough to warrant a discussion and investigation.

If you wish to make the most of your individuality, go before your audience rested. A tired man is not magnetic nor attractive. Don't make the all-too-common error of putting off your preparation and your planning until the very last moment, and then working at a furious pace, trying to make up for lost time. If you do, you are bound to store up bodily poisons and brain fatigues that will prove terrific drags, holding you down, sapping your vitality, weakening both your brain and your nerves.

If you must make an important talk to a committee meeting at four, do not, if you can well avoid it, come back to the office after lunch. Go home, if possible, have a light lunch and the refreshment of a siesta. Rest—that is what you need—physical and mental and nervous.

When you have to make an important talk, beware of your hunger. Eat as sparingly as a saint. On Sunday afternoons, Henry Ward Beecher used to have biscuits and milk at five, and nothing after that.

"When I am singing in the evening," said Madame Melba, "I do not dine but have a very light repast at five o'clock, consisting of either fish, chicken, or sweetbread, with a baked apple and a glass of water. I always find myself very hungry for supper when I get home from the opera or concert."

How wisely Melba and Beecher acted, I never realized until after I became a professional speaker myself and tried to deliver a two-hour talk each evening having consumed a hearty meal.

Experience taught me that I couldn't enjoy a *filet de sole aux pommes nature* and follow that by a beef-steak and fried potatoes and salad and vegetables and a sweet, and then stand up an hour afterwards and do either myself or my subject or my body justice. The blood that ought to have been in my brain was down in my stomach wrestling with that steak and potatoes. Paderewski was right: he said when he ate what he wanted to eat before a concert, the animal in him got uppermost, that it even got into his fingertips and clogged and dulled his playing.

WHAT MAKES A GOOD SPEAKER

Do nothing to dull your energy. It is magnetic. Vitality, aliveness, enthusiasm: they are among the first qualities I have always sought for in employing speakers and instructors of speaking. People cluster around the energetic speaker, the human dynamo of energy, like wild geese around a field of autumn wheat.

I have often seen this illustrated by the open air speakers in Hyde Park, London. A spot near Marble Arch entrance is a rendezvous for speakers of every creed and colour. On a Sunday afternoon, one can take his choice and listen to a Catholic explaining the doctrine of the infallibility of the Pope, to a Socialist propounding the economic gospel of Karl Marx, to an Indian explaining why it is right and proper for a Mohammedan to have four wives, and so on. Hundreds crowd about one speaker, while his neighbor has only a handful. Why? Is the topic always an adequate explanation of the disparity between the drawing powers of different speakers? No. More often the explanation is to be found in the speaker himself: he is more interested and, consequently, interesting. He talks with more life and spirit. He radiates vitality and animation; they always challenge attention.

THE IMPORTANCE OF GROOMING

An inquiry was sent to a large group of people by a psychologist and university president, asking them the impression clothes made on them. All but unanimously, they testified that when they were well groomed and faultlessly and immaculately attired, the knowledge of it, the feeling of it, had an effect which, while it was difficult to explain, was still very definite, very real. It gave them more confidence, brought them increased faith in themselves, and heightened their self-respect. They declared that when they had the look of success they found it easier to think success, to achieve success. Such is the effect of clothes on the wearer himself.

What effect do they have on an audience? I have noticed time and again that if a speaker has baggy trousers, shapeless coat and footwear, fountain pen and pencils peeping out of his breast pocket, a newspaper or a pipe and tin of tobacco bulging out the sides of his garment—I have noticed that an audience has as little respect for that man as he has for his own appearance. Aren't they very likely to assume that his mind is as sloppy as his unkempt hair and unpolished shoes?

BEING IN THE SPOTLIGHT

When General Lee came to Appomattox Court House to surrender his army, he was immaculately attired in a new uniform and, at his side, hung a sword of extraordinary value. Grant was coatless, swordless, and was wearing the shirt and trousers of a private. "I must have contrasted very strangely," he wrote in his *Memoirs,* "with a man so handsomely dressed, six feet high, and of faultless form." The fact that he had not been appropriately attired for this historic occasion came to be one of the real regrets of Grant's life.

The Department of Agriculture has several hundred stands of bees on its experimental farm. Each hive has a large magnifying glass built into it, and the interior can be flooded with electric light by pressing a button; so, any moment, night or day, these bees are liable to be subject to the minutest scrutiny. A speaker is like that: he is under the magnifying glass, he is in the spotlight, all eyes are upon him. The smallest disharmony in his personal appearance now looms up like a mountain from the plains.

"HE WHO CANNOT SMILE OUGHT NOT TO KEEP A SHOP"

A number of years ago, I was writing the life story of a certain banker for a magazine. I asked one of his friends to explain the reason for his success. No small amount of it, he said, was due to the man's winning smile. At first thought, that may sound like exaggeration but I believe it is really true. Other men, scores of them, hundreds of them, may have had more experience and as good financial judgment, but he had an additional asset they didn't possess—he had a most agreeable personality. And a warm, welcoming smile was one of the striking features of it. It gained one's confidence immediately. It secured one's goodwill instantly. We all want to see a man like that succeed, and it is a real pleasure to give him our patronage.

"He who cannot smile," says a Chinese proverb, "ought not to keep a shop." And isn't a smile just as welcome before an audience as behind a counter? I am thinking now of a particular student who attended a course in public speaking conducted by a Chamber of Commerce. He always came out before the audience with an air that said he liked to be there, that he loved the job that was before him. He always smiled and acted as if he were glad to see us, and so immediately and inevitably his hearers warmed towards him and welcomed him.

But I have seen speakers—students of this course, I regret to admit—who walked out before the other members in a cold, perfunctory manner as if they had a disagreeable task to perform, and that, when it was over, they would thank God. We in the audience were soon feeling the same way. These attitudes are contagious.

SEAT YOUR AUDIENCE TOGETHER

As a public lecturer, I have frequently spoken to a small audience scattered through a large hall in the afternoon, and to a large audience packed into the same hall at night. The evening audience has laughed heartily at the same things that brought only a smile to the faces of the afternoon group; the evening crowd has applauded generously at the very places where the afternoon gathering was utterly unresponsive. Why?

For one thing, the elderly women and the children that are likely to come in the afternoon cannot be expected to be as demonstrative as the more vigorous and discriminating evening crowd; but that is only a partial explanation.

The fact is that no audience will be easily moved when it is scattered. Nothing so dampens enthusiasm as wide, open spaces and empty chairs between the listeners.

Henry Ward Beecher said in his *Lectures on Preaching:*

People often say, "Do you not think it is much more inspiring to speak to a large audience than a small one?" No, I say. I can speak just as well to twelve persons as to a thousand, provided those twelve are crowded around me and close together, so that they can touch each other. But even a thousand people with four feet of space between every two of them, would be just the same as an empty room… Crowd your audience together and you will set them off with half the effort.

A man in a large audience tends to lose his individuality. He becomes a member of the crowd and is swayed far more easily than he would be as a single individual. He will laugh at and applaud things that would leave him unmoved if he were only one of half a dozen people listening to you.

It is far easier to get people to act as a body than to act singly. Men going into battle, for example, invariably want to do the most dangerous and reckless thing in the world—they want to huddle together. During the late war, German soldiers were known to go into battle at times with their arms locked about one another.

Crowds! Crowds! Crowds! They are a curious phenomenon. All great popular movements and reforms have been carried forward by the aid of the crowd mentality. An interesting book on this subject is Everett Dean Martin's *The Behaviour of Crowds*.

If we are going to talk to a small group, we should choose a small room. Better to pack the aisles of a small place than to have people scattered through the lonely, deadening spaces of a large hall.

If your hearers are scattered, ask them to move down front and be seated near you. Insist on this, before you start speaking.

Unless the audience is a fairly large one, and there is a real reason, a necessity, for the speaker standing on a platform, don't do so. Get down on the same level with them. Stand near them. Break up all formality. Get an intimate contact. Make the thing conversational.

OPEN THE WINDOWS

Keep the air fresh. In the well-known process of public speaking, oxygen is just as essential as the larynx, pharynx and human epiglottis. All the eloquence of Cicero, and all the feminine pulchritude in Ziegfeld's Follies, could hardly keep an audience awake in a room poisoned with bad air. So, when I am one of a number of speakers, before beginning, I almost always ask the audience to stand up and rest for two minutes while the windows are thrown open.

For fourteen years Major James B. Pond traveled all over the United States and Canada as manager for Henry Ward Beecher when that famous preacher was at his flood tide as a popular lecturer. Before the audience assembled, Pond always visited the hall or church or theatre where Beecher was to appear, and rigorously inspected the lighting, seating, temperature and ventilation. Pond had been a blustering, roaring old army officer and he loved to exercise authority; so if the place was too warm or the air was dead and he could not get the windows open, he hurled books through them, smashing and shattering the glass. He believed with Spurgeon that "the next best thing to the Grace of God for a preacher is oxygen".

LET LIGHT SHINE ON YOUR FACE

Unless you are demonstrating spiritualism before a group of

people, flood the room, if possible, with lights. It is as easy to domesticate a quail as to develop enthusiasm in a half-lighted room gloomy as the inside of a thermos bottle.

Read David Belasco's articles on stage production, and you will discover that the average speaker does not have the foggiest shadow of the ghost of an idea of the tremendous importance of proper lighting.

Let the light strike your face. People want to see you. The subtle changes that ought to play across your features are a part, and a very real part, of the process of self-expression. Sometimes they mean more than your words. If you stand directly under a light, your face may be dimmed by a shadow; if you stand directly in front of a light, it is sure to be. Would it not, then, be the part of wisdom to select, before you arise to speak, the spot that will give you the most advantageous illumination?

NO TRUMPERY ON THE PLATFORM

And do not hide behind a table. People want to look at the whole man. They will even lean out in the aisles to see all of him.

Some well-meaning soul is pretty sure to give you a table and a water pitcher and a glass; but if your throat becomes dry, a pinch of salt or a taste of lemon will start the saliva again better than Niagara.

You do not want the water nor the pitcher. Neither do you want all the other useless and ugly impedimenta that clutter up the average platform.

The sales rooms of the various automobile makers are beautiful, orderly, pleasing to the eye. The Paris offices of the large perfumers and jewelers are artistically and luxuriously appointed. Why? It is good business. One has more respect, more confidence, more admiration for a concern housed like that.

For the same reason, a speaker ought to have a pleasing background. The ideal arrangement, to my way of thinking, would be no furniture at all. Nothing behind the speaker to attract attention or at either side of him—nothing but a curtain of dark blue velvet.

But what does he usually have behind him? Maps and signs and tables, perhaps a lot of dusty chairs, some piled on top of the others. And what is the result? A cheap, slovenly, disorderly atmosphere. So clear all the trumpery away.

"The most important thing in public speaking," said Henry Ward Beecher, "is the man."

So let the man stand out like the snow clad top of the Jungfrau towering against the blue skies of Switzerland.

NO GUESTS ON THE PLATFORM

I was once in London, Ontario, when the Prime Minister of Canada was speaking. Presently the janitor, armed with a long pole, started to ventilate the room, moving about from window to window. What happened? The audience, almost to a man, ignored the speaker for a little while and stared at the janitor as intently as if he had been performing some miracle.

An audience cannot resist—or, what comes to the same thing, it *will not* resist—the temptation to look at moving objects. If a speaker will only remember that truth, he can save himself some trouble and needless annoyance.

First, he can refrain from twiddling his thumbs, playing with his clothes and making little nervous movements that detract from him. I remember seeing a New York audience watch a well-known speaker's hands for half an hour while he spoke and played with the covering of a pulpit at the same time.

Second, the speaker should arrange, if possible, to have the audience seated so they won't have their attention distracted by seeing the latecomers enter.

Third, he should have no guests on the platform. A few years ago Raymond Robins delivered a series of talks. I, along with a number of others, was invited to sit on the platform with him. I declined on the ground that it was unfair to the speaker. I noted the first night how many of these guests shifted about and put one leg over the other and back again, and so on; and every time one of them moved, the audience looked away from the speaker to the guest. I called Mr. Robins' attention to this the next day; and during the remainder of his evenings with us, he very wisely occupied the platform alone.

David Belasco did not permit the use of red flowers on the stage because they attract too much attention. Then why should a speaker permit a restless human being to sit facing the audience while he talks? He shouldn't. And, if he is wise, he won't.

THE ART OF SITTING DOWN

Isn't it well for the speaker himself not to sit facing the audience before he begins? Isn't it better to arrive as a fresh exhibit than an old one?

But, if we *must* sit, let us be careful of *how* we sit. You have seen men look round to find a chair with the modified movements of a foxhound lying down for the night. They turned round and when they did locate a chair, they doubled up and flopped down into it with all the self-control of a sack of sand.

A man who knows how to sit feels the chair strike the back

of his legs, and, with his body easily erect from head to hips, he *sinks* into it with his body under perfect control.

POISE

We just said, a few pages previously, not to play with your clothes because it attracted attention. There is another reason also. It gives an impression of weakness, a lack of self-control. Every movement that does not add to your presence detracts from it. There are no neutral movements. None. So stand still and control yourself physically and that will give you an impression of mental control, of poise.

After you have risen to address your audience, do not be in a hurry to begin. That is the hallmark of the amateur. Take a deep breath. Look over your audience for a moment; and, if there is a noise or disturbance, pause until it quiets down.

Hold your chest high. But why wait until you get before an audience to do this? Why not do it daily in private? Then you will do it unconsciously in public.

"Not one man in ten," says Luther H. Gulick in his book *The Efficient Light,* "carries himself so as to look his best... Keep the neck pressed against the collar." Here is a daily exercise he recommends: "Inhale slowly and as strongly as possible. At the same time press the neck back firmly against the collar. Now hold it there hard. There is no harm in doing this in an exaggerated way. The object is to "straighten out that part of the back which is directly between the shoulders. This deepens the chest."

And what shall you do with your hands? Forget them. If they fall naturally to your sides, that is ideal. If they feel like a bunch of bananas to you, do not be deluded into imagining that anyone else is paying the slightest attention to them or has the slightest interest in them.

They will look best hanging relaxed at your sides. They will attract the minimum of attention there. Not even the hypercritical can criticize that position. Besides, they will be unhampered and free to flow naturally into gestures when the urge makes itself felt.

But suppose that you are very nervous and that you find putting them behind your back or shoving them into your pockets helps to relieve your self-consciousness—what should you do? Use your common sense. I have heard a number of celebrated speakers of this generation. Many, if not most, put their hands into their pockets occasionally while speaking. Bryan did it. Chauncey M. Depew did it. Teddy Roosevelt did it. Even so fastidious a dandy as Disraeli sometimes succumbed to this temptation. But the sky did not fall and, according to the weather reports, if my memory serves me right, the sun came up on time as usual the next morning. If a man has something to say worthwhile, and says it with contagious conviction, surely it will matter little what he does with his hands and feet. If his head is full and heart stirred, these secondary details will very largely take care of themselves. After all, the stupendously important thing in making a talk is the psychological aspect of it, not the position of the hands and feet.

ABSURD ANTICS TAUGHT IN THE NAME OF GESTURE

And this brings us very naturally to the much-abused question of gesture. My first lesson in public speaking was given by the president of a college in the middle west. This lesson, as I remember it, was chiefly concerned with gesturing; it was not only useless but misleading and positively harmful. I was taught to let my arm hang loosely at my side palm facing the rear, fingers half closed and thumb touching my leg. I was drilled to bring the arm up in a graceful curve, to make a classical swing with the wrist and then to unfold the forefinger first, the second finger next, and the little finger last. When the whole aesthetic and ornamental movement had been executed, the arm was then to retrace the same graceful and unnatural curve and rest again by the side of the leg. The whole performance was wooden and affected. There was nothing sensible or honest about it. I was drilled to act as no man in his right mind ever acted anywhere.

There was no attempt whatever to get me to put my own individuality into my movements; no attempt to spur me on to feeling like gesturing; no endeavor to get the flow and blood of life in the process, and make it natural and unconscious and inevitable; no urging me to let go, to be spontaneous, to break through my shell of reserve, to talk and act like a human being. No, the whole regrettable performance was as mechanical as a typewriter, as lifeless as a last year's bird nest, as ridiculous as a Punch and Judy show.

That was in 1902. It seems incredible that such absurd antics could have been taught in the twentieth century, but they are still going on. Only a few years ago a whole book about gesturing was published by a professor teaching in one of the large colleges of the East—a whole book trying to make automatons out of men, telling them which gesture to make on this sentence, which to make on that, which to make with one hand, which with both, which to make high, which to make medium, which to make low, how to hold this finger and how to hold that. I have seen twenty men at a time standing before a class, all reading the same ornate oratorical selections from such a book, all making precisely the same gestures on precisely the same words, and all making themselves precisely ridiculous. Artificial, time-killing, mechanical, injurious—it has brought this whole subject into disrepute with many men. The dean of a large college in Massachusetts recently said that his institution had no course in public speaking because he had never seen one that was practical, one that taught men to speak sensibly. My sympathy was all with the dean.

Nine-tenths of the stuff that has been written on gestures has been a waste and worse than a waste of good white paper and good black ink. Any gesture out of a book is very likely to look like it. The place to get it is out of yourself, out of your heart out of your mind, out of your own interest in the subject, out of your own desire to make someone else see as you see, out of your own impulses. The only gestures that are worth one, two, three, are those that are born on the spur of the instant. An ounce of spontaneity is worth a ton of rules.

Gesture is not a thing to be put on at will like a dinner jacket. It is merely an outward expression of inward condition just as are kisses and colic and laughter and sea sickness.

And a man's gestures, like his toothbrush, should be very personal things. And, as all men are different, their gestures will be individual if they will only act naturally.

No two men should be drilled to gesture in precisely the same fashion. In the last chapter, I discussed the difference between Lincoln and Douglas as speakers. Imagine trying to make the long, awkward, slow-thinking Lincoln gesture in the same fashion as did the rapidly-talking, impetuous and polished Douglas. It would be ridiculous.

"Lincoln," according to his biographer and law partner, Herndon, "did not gesticulate as much with his hands as with his head. He used the latter frequently, throwing it with vim this way and that. This movement was a significant one when he sought to enforce his statement. It sometimes came with a quick jerk, as if throwing off electric sparks into combustible material. He never sawed the air or rent space into tatters and rags as some orators do. He never acted for stage effect... As he moved along in his speech, he became freer and less uneasy in his movements; to that extent he was graceful. He had a perfect naturalness, a strong individuality, and to that extent he was dignified. He despised glitter, show, set forms, and shams... There was a world of meaning and emphasis in the long, bony finger of his right hand as he dotted the ideas on the minds of his hearers. Sometimes, to express joy or pleasure, he would raise both hands at an angle of about fifty degrees, the palms upward, as if desirous of embracing the spirit of that which he loved. If the sentiment was one of detestation—denunciation of slavery, for example—both arms, thrown upward and fists clenched, swept through the air, and he expressed an execration that was truly sublime. This was one of his most effective gestures, and signified most vividly a fixed determination to drag down the object of his hatred and trample it in the dust. He always stood squarely on his feet, toe even with toe; that is, he never put one foot before the other. He neither touched nor leaned on anything for support. He made but few changes in his positions and attitudes. He never ranted, never walked backward and forward on the platform. To ease his arms, he frequently caught hold, with his left hand of the lapel of his coat, keeping his thumb upright and leaving his right hand free to gesticulate." St. Gaudens caught him in just that attitude in the statue facing Westminster Abbey.

Such was Lincoln's method. Theodore Roosevelt was more vigorous, fiery, active, his whole face alive with feeling, his fist clenched, his entire body an instrument of expression. Bryan often used the outstretched hand with open palm. Gladstone often struck a table or his open palm with his fist, or stamped his foot with a resounding thud on the floor. Lord Rosebery used to raise his right arm and bring it down with a bold sweep that had tremendous force. Ah, but there was force first in the speaker's thoughts and convictions; that was what made the gesture strong and spontaneous.

Spontaneity…life…they are the *summum bonum* of action. Burke was angular and exceedingly awkward in his gestures. Pitt sawed the air with his arms "like a clumsy clown". Sir Henry Irving was handicapped by a lame leg and decidedly odd movements. Lord Macaulay's actions on the platform were ungainly. So were Grattan's. So were Parnell's. "The answer then appears to be," said the late Lord Curzon at Cambridge University, in an address on Parliamentary Eloquence, "that great public speakers make their own gestures; and that while a great orator is doubtless aided by a handsome exterior and graceful action, it does not matter very much if he happens to be ugly and awkward."

Some years ago, I heard the famous Gypsy Smith preach. I was enthralled by the eloquence of this man who has led so many thousands to Christ. He used gestures—lots of them—and was no more conscious of them than of the air he breathed. Such is the ideal way.

And such is the way you, my dear reader, will find yourself making gestures if you will but practice and apply the principles already enunciated in this course. I can't give you any rules for gesturing, for everything depends upon the temperament of the speaker, upon his preparation, his enthusiasm, his personality, the subject, the audience, the occasion.

SOME SUGGESTIONS

Here are, however, a few limited suggestions that may prove useful. Do not repeat one gesture until it becomes monotonous.

Do not make short, jerky movements from the elbow. The movements from the shoulder look better on the platform. Do not end your gestures too quickly. If you are using the index finger to drive home your thought, do not be afraid to hold that gesture through an entire sentence. The failure to do this is a very common error and a serious one. It distorts your emphasis, making small things unimportant, and truly important points seem trivial by comparison.

When you are doing real speaking before a real audience, make only the gestures that come natural. But while you are practicing before the members of this course, *force* yourself, if necessary, to use gestures. Force yourself to do it and the doing of it will so awaken and stimulate you that your gestures will soon be coming unsought.

Shut your book. You can't learn gestures from a printed page. Your own impulses, as you are speaking, are more to be trusted, more valuable than anything any instructor can possibly tell you.

If you forget all else we have said about gesture and delivery, remember this: if a man is so wrapped up in what he has to say, if he is so eager to get his message across that he forgets himself and talks and acts spontaneously, then his gestures and his delivery, unstudied though they may be, are very likely to be almost above criticism. If you doubt this, walk up to a man and knock him down. You will probably discover that, when he regains his feet, the talk he delivers will be well nigh flawless as a gem of eloquence.

Here are the best eleven words I have ever read on the subject of delivery:

> Fill up the barrel.
> Knock out the bung.
> Let nature caper.

POINTS TO REMEMBER

1. Personality is the most important factor in public address.
2. Don't make the all-too-common error of putting off your preparation and your planning until the very last moment.
3. Your outward gestures should always be spontaneous.

9

SELF-CONFIDENCE THROUGH PREPARATION

It has been my professional duty as well as pleasure to listen to and criticize approximately six thousand speeches a year each season since 1912. These were made, not by college students, but by mature business and professional men. If that experience has engraved on my mind any one thing more deeply than another, surely it is this: the urgent necessity of preparing a talk before one starts to make it and of having something clear and definite to say, something that has impressed one, something that won't stay unsaid. Aren't you unconsciously drawn to the speaker who, you feel, has a real message in his head and heart that he zealously desires to communicate to your head and heart? That is half the secret of speaking.

When a speaker is in that kind of mental and emotional state he will discover a significant fact: namely, that his talk will almost make itself. Its yoke will be easy, its burden will be light. A well-prepared speech is already nine-tenths delivered.

The primary reason why most men take this course, is to acquire confidence and courage and self-reliance. And the one fatal mistake many make is neglecting to prepare their talks. How can they even hope to subdue the cohorts of fear, the cavalry of nervousness, when they go into the battle with wet powder and blank shells, or with no ammunition at all? Under the circumstances, small wonder that they are not exactly at home before an audience. "I believe," said Lincoln in the White House, "that I shall never be old enough to speak without embarrassment when I have nothing to say."

If you want confidence, why not do the things necessary to bring it about?

Why don't those enrolled in this course prepare their talks more carefully? Why? Some don't clearly understand what preparation is nor how to go about it wisely; others plead a lack of time. So we shall discuss these problems rather fully—and we trust lucidly and profitably—in this chapter.

THE RIGHT WAY TO PREPARE

What is preparation? Reading a book? That is one kind, but not the best. Reading may help; but if one attempts to lift a lot of "canned" thoughts out of a book and to give them out immediately as his own, the whole performance will be lacking in something. The audience may not know precisely what is lacking, but they will not warm to the speaker.

To illustrate: some time ago I conducted a course in public speaking for the senior officers of banks. Naturally, the members of such a group, having many demands upon their time, frequently found it difficult to prepare adequately or to do what they conceived of as preparing. All their lives they had been thinking their own individual thoughts, nurturing their own personal convictions, seeing things from their own distinctive angles, living their own original experiences. So, in that fashion they had spent forty years storing up material for speeches. But it was hard for some of them to realize that.

They could not see the forest for "the murmuring pines and the hemlocks".

This group met Friday evenings from five to seven. One Friday, a certain gentleman connected with a bank—for our purposes here, we shall designate him as Mr. Jackson—found four-thirty had arrived, and, what was he to talk about? He walked out of his office, bought a copy of a magazine at a news stand and, in the subway coming down to the bank where the class met, he read an article entitled, "You Have Only Ten Years to Succeed". He read it not because he was interested in the article especially, but because he must speak on something, on anything, to fill his quota of time.

An hour later, he stood up and attempted to talk convincingly and interestingly on the contents of this article.

What was the result, the inevitable result?

He had not digested, had not assimilated what he was trying to say. "Trying to say"—that expresses it precisely. He was *trying*. There was no real message in him seeking for an outlet, and his whole manner and tone revealed it unmistakably. How could he expect the audience to be any more impressed than he himself was? He kept referring to the article saying the author said so and so. There was a surfeit of the magazine in it, but regrettably little of Mr. Jackson.

So I addressed him somewhat in this fashion: "Mr. Jackson, we are not interested in this shadowy personality who wrote that article. He is not here. We can't see him. But we are interested in you and your ideas. Tell us what you think, personally, not what somebody else said. Put more of Mr. Jackson in this. Why not take this same subject for next week? Why not read this article again, and ask yourself whether you agree with the author or not? If you do, think out his suggestions and illustrate them with observations from your own experience. If you don't agree with him, say so and tell us why. Let this article be merely the starting point from which you launch your own speech."

Mr. Jackson accepted the suggestion, reread the article and concluded that he did not agree with the author at all. He did not sit down in the subway and try to prepare this next speech to order. He let it grow. It was a child of his own brain, and it developed and expanded and took on stature just as his physical children had done. And like his daughters, this other child grew day and night when he was least conscious of it. One thought was suggested to him while reading some item in the newspaper, another illustration swam into his mind unexpectedly when he was discussing the subject with a friend. The thing deepened and heightened, lengthened and thickened, as he thought over it during the odd moments of the week.

The next time Mr. Jackson spoke on this subject, he had something that was his, ore that he dug out of his own mine, currency coined in his own mint. And he spoke all the better because he was disagreeing with the author of the article. There is no spur to rouse one like a little opposition.

What an incredible contrast between these two speeches by the same man, in the same fortnight, on the same subject. What a colossal difference the right kind of preparation makes!

Let us cite another illustration of how to do it and how not to do it. A gentleman, whom we shall call Mr. Flynn, was a student of this course. One afternoon he devoted his talk to eulogizing his home tour. He had hastily and superficially gleaned his facts from a tourist booklet. They sounded like it—dry, disconnected, undigested. He had not thought over his subject adequately. It had not elicited his enthusiasm. He did not feel what he was saying deeply enough to make it worth while expressing. The whole affair was flat and flavourless and unprofitable.

A fortnight later something happened that touched Mr. Flynn to the core: a thief stole his motorcar out of a public garage. He rushed to the police and offered rewards, but it was all in vain. The police admitted that it was well nigh impossible for them to cope with the crime situation; yet, only a week previously, they had found time to walk about the street, chalk in hand, and fine Mr. Flynn because he had parked his car fifteen minutes at a kerb. These "chalk cops", who were so busy annoying respectable citizens that they could not catch criminals, aroused his ire. He was indignant. He had something now to say, not something that he had got out of a book, but something that was leaping hot out of his own life and experience. Here was something that was part and parcel of the real man—something that had aroused his feelings and convictions. In his speech eulogizing the city, he had laboriously pulled out sentence by sentence; but now he had but to stand on his feet and open his mouth, and his condemnation of the police welled up and boiled forth like Vesuvius in action. A speech like that is almost foolproof. It can hardly fail. It was experience plus reflection.

WHAT IS MEANT BY PREPARATION

Does the preparation of a speech mean the getting together of some faultless phrases written down or memorized? No. Does it mean the assembling of a few casual thoughts that really convey very little to you personally? Not at all. It means the assembling of *your* thoughts, *your* ideas, *your* convictions, *your* urges. And you have such thoughts, such urges. You have them every day of your waking life. They even swarm through your dreams. Your whole existence has been filled with feelings and experiences. These things are lying deep in your subconscious mind as thick as pebbles on the seashore. Preparation means thinking, brooding, recalling, selecting the ones that appeal to you most, polishing them, working them into a pattern, a mosaic of your own. That doesn't sound like such a difficult programme, does it? It isn't. It just requires a little concentration and thinking to a purpose.

THE SAGE ADVICE OF DEAN BROWN OF YALE

A few years ago the Yale Divinity School celebrated the one hundredth anniversary of its founding. On that occasion, the Dean, Dr. Charles Reynold Brown, delivered a series of lectures on the Art of Preaching. These are now published in book form under that name by the Macmillan Company, New York. Dr. Brown has been preparing addresses himself weekly for a third of a century, and also training others to prepare and deliver; so he was in a position to dispense some sage advice on the subject, advice that will hold good regardless of whether the speaker is a man of the cloth preparing a discourse on the Ninety-first Psalm, or a shoe manufacturer preparing a speech on Labour Unions. So I am taking the liberty of quoting Dr. Brown here:

> Brood over your text and your topic. Brood over them until they become mellow and responsive. You will hatch out of them a whole flock of promising ideas as you cause the tiny germs of life there contained to expand and develop...
>
> It will be all the better if this process can go on for a long time and not be postponed until Saturday afternoon when you are actually making your final preparation for Sunday. If a minister can hold a certain truth in his mind for a month, for six months perhaps, for a

year it may be before he preaches on it he will find new ideas perpetually sprouting out of it, until it shows an abundant growth. He may meditate on it as he walks the streets, or as he spends some hours on a train, when his eyes are too tired to read.

He may indeed brood upon it in the night-time. It is better for the minister not to take his church or his sermon to bed with him habitually—a pulpit is a splendid thing to preach from, but it is not a good bedfellow. Yet, for all that, I have sometimes got out of bed in the middle of the night to put down the thoughts which came to me, for fear I might forget them before morning....

When you are actually engaged in assembling the material for a particular sermon, write down everything that comes to you bearing upon that text and topic. Write down what you saw in the text when you first chose it. Write down all the associated ideas which now occur to you...

Put all these ideas of yours down in writing, just a few words, enough to fix the idea, and keep your mind reaching for more all the time as if it were never to see another book as long as it lived. This is the way to train the mind in productiveness. You will by this method keep your own mental processes fresh, original, creative...

Put down all of those ideas which you have brought to the birth yourself, unaided. They are more precious for your mental unfolding than rubies and diamonds and much fine gold. Put them down, preferably on scraps of paper, backs of old letters, fragments of envelopes, waste paper, anything which comes to your hand. This is much better in every way than to use nice, long, clean sheets of foolscap. It is not a mere matter of economy—you will find it easier to arrange and organize these loose bits when you come to set your material in order.

Keep on putting down all the ideas which come to your mind, thinking hard all the while. You need not hurry this process. It is one of the most important mental transactions in which you will be privileged to engage. It is this method which causes the mind to grow in real productive power…

You will find that the sermons you enjoy preaching the most and the ones which actually accomplish the most good in the lives of your people will be those sermons which you take most largely out of your own interiors. They are bone of your bone, flesh of your flesh, the children of your own mental labour, the output of your own creative energy. The sermons which are garbled and compiled will always have a kind of second-hand, warmed-over flavor about them. The sermons which live and move and enter into the temple, walking and leaping and praising God, the sermons which enter into the hearts of men causing them to mount up with wings like eagles and to walk in the way of duty and not faint—these real sermons are the ones which are actually born from the vital energies of the man who utters them.

HOW LINCOLN PREPARED HIS SPEECHES

How did Lincoln prepare his speeches? Fortunately, we know the facts and, as you read here of his method, you will observe that Dean Brown, in his lecture, commended several of the procedures that Lincoln had employed three-quarters of a century previously. One of Lincoln's most famous addresses was that in which he declared with prophetic vision: "A house divided against itself cannot stand. I believe this government cannot endure, permanently, half-slave and half-free." This speech was thought out as he went about his usual work, as he ate his meals, as he walked the street, as he sat in his barn milking his cow, as he made his daily trip to the butcher shop and grocery, an old grey shawl over his shoulders, his market basket over his arm, his little son at his side, chattering and questioning, growing peeved, and jerking at the long bony fingers in a vain effort to make his father talk to him. But Lincoln stalked on, absorbed in his own reflections, thinking of his speech, apparently unconscious of the boy's existence.

From time to time during this brooding and hatching process, he jotted down notes, fragments, sentences here and there on stray envelopes, scraps of paper, bits torn from paper sacks—anything that was near. These he stowed away in the top of his hat and carried them there until he was ready to sit down and arrange them in order, and to write and revise the whole thing, and to shape it up for delivery and publication.

In the joint debates of 1858, Senator Douglas delivered the same speech wherever he went; but Lincoln kept studying and contemplating and reflecting until he found it easier, he said, to make a new speech each day than to repeat an old one. The subject was for ever widening and enlarging in his mind.

A short time before he moved into the White House, he took a copy of the Constitution and three speeches, and with only these for reference, he locked himself in a dingy, dusty back room over a store in Springfield; and there, away from all intrusion and interruption, he wrote out his inaugural address.

How did Lincoln prepare his Gettysburg address? Unfortunately, false reports have been circulated about it. The true story, however, is fascinating. Let us have it:

When the commission in charge of the Gettysburg cemetery decided to arrange for a formal dedication, they invited Edward

Everett to deliver the speech. He had been a Boston minister, President of Harvard, Governor of Massachusetts, United States Senator, Minister to England, Secretary of State, and was generally considered to be America's most capable speaker. The date first set for the dedication ceremonies was October 23, 1863. Mr. Everett very wisely declared that it would be impossible for him to prepare adequately on such short notice. So the dedication was postponed until November 19, nearly a month, to give him time to prepare. The last three days of that period he spent in Gettysburg, going over the battlefield, familiarizing himself with all that had taken place there. That period of brooding and thinking was most excellent preparation. It made the battle real to him.

Invitations to be present were despatched to all the members of Congress, to the President and his cabinet. Most of these declined; the committee was surprised when Lincoln agreed to come. Should they ask him to speak? They had not intended to do so. Objections were raised. He would not have time to prepare. Besides, even if he did have time, had he the ability? True, he could handle himself well in a debate on slavery; but no one had ever heard him deliver a dedicatory address. This was a grave and solemn occasion. They ought not to take any chances. Should they ask him to speak? They wondered, wondered… But they would have wondered a thousand times more had they been able to look into the future and to see that this man, whose ability they were questioning, was to deliver on that occasion what is very generally accepted now as one of the most enduring addresses ever delivered by the lips of mortal man.

Finally, a fortnight before the event, they sent Lincoln a belated invitation to make "a few appropriate remarks". Yes, that is the way they worded it: "a few appropriate remarks". Think of writing that to the President of the United States!

Lincoln immediately set about preparing. He wrote to Edward Everett, secured a copy of the address that that classic scholar was to deliver and, a day or two later, going to a photographer's gallery to pose for his photograph, Lincoln took Everett's manuscript with him and read it during the spare time that he had at the studio. He thought over his talk for days, thought over it while walking back and forth between the White House and the War Office, thought over it while he stretched out on a leather couch in the War Office waiting for the late telegraphic reports. He wrote a rough draft of it on a piece of foolscap paper, and carried it about in the top of his tall silk hat. Ceaselessly he was brooding over it, ceaselessly it was taking shape. The Sunday before it was delivered he said to Noah Brooks: "It is not exactly written. It is not finished anyway. I have written it over two or three times, and I shall have to give it another lick before I am satisfied."

He arrived in Gettysburg the night before the dedication. The little town was filled to overflowing. Its usual population of thirteen hundred had suddenly swelled to fifteen thousand. The pavements became clogged, impassable, men and women took to the dirt streets. Half a dozen bands were playing; crowds were singing "John Brown's Body". People foregathered before the home of Mr. Wills where Lincoln was being entertained. They serenaded him; they demanded a speech. Lincoln responded with a few words which conveyed with more clearness than tact, perhaps, that he was unwilling to speak until the morrow. The facts are that he was spending the latter part of that evening giving his speech "another lick". He even went to an adjoining house where Secretary Seward was staying and read the speech aloud to him for his criticism. After breakfast the next morning, he continued "to give it another lick", working on it until a rap came at the door informing him that it was time for him to take his place in the procession. "Colonel Carr, who rode just behind the President, stated that when the procession started, the President sat erect on his horse, and looked the part of the commander-in-chief of the army; but, as the procession moved on, his body leaned forward, his arms hung limp, and his head was bowed. He seemed absorbed in thought."

We can only guess that even then he was going over his little speech of ten immortal sentences, giving it "another lick".

Some of Lincoln's speeches, in which he had only a superficial interest, were unquestioned failures, but he was possessed of extraordinary power when he spoke of slavery and the union. Why? Because he thought ceaselessly on these problems and felt deeply. A companion who shared a room with him one night in an Illinois tavern awoke next morning at daylight to find Lincoln sitting up in bed, staring at the wall, and his first words were: "This government cannot endure permanently, half-slave and half-free."

How did Christ prepare His addresses? He withdrew from the crowd. He thought. He brooded. He pondered. He went out alone into the wilderness and meditated and fasted for forty days and forty nights. "From that time on," records Saint Matthew, "Jesus began to preach." Shortly after that, He delivered one of the world's most celebrated speeches: the Sermon on the Mount.

"That is all very interesting," you may protest, "but I have no desire to become an immortal orator. I merely want to make a few simple talks in business occasionally."

True, and we realize your wants fully. This course is for the specific purpose of helping you and other businessmen like you to do just that. But, unpretending as the talks of yours may prove to be, you can profit by and utilize in some measure the methods of the famous speakers of the past.

HOW TO PREPARE YOUR TALK

What topics ought you to speak on during the sessions of this course? Anything that interests you. If possible, choose your own topics; you will be more fortunate still if your topic chooses you. However, you will often have topics suggested for you by your instructor.

Don't make the almost universal mistake of trying to cover too much ground in a brief talk. Just take one or two angles of a subject and attempt to cover them adequately. You will be fortunate if you can do that in the short speeches that are necessitated by the time schedule of this course.

Determine your subject a week in advance so that you will have time to think it over in odd moments. Think it over for seven days; dream over it for seven nights. Think of it the last thing when you retire. Think of it the next morning while you are shaving, while you are bathing, while you are riding downtown, while you are waiting for lifts, for lunch, for appointments. Discuss it with your friends. Make it a topic of conversation.

Ask yourself all possible questions concerning it. If, for example, you are to speak on divorce, ask yourself what causes divorce, what are the effects economically, socially. How can the evil be remedied? Should divorce be made impossible? More difficult? Easier?

Suppose you were going to talk on why you enrolled for this course. You ought then to ask yourself such questions as these: What are my troubles? What do I hope to get out of this instruction? Have I ever made a public talk? If so, when? Where? What happened? Why do I think this training is valuable for a businessman? Do I know men who are forging ahead commercially largely because of their self-confidence, their presence, their ability to talk convincingly? Do I know others who will probably never achieve a gratifying measure of success because they lack these positive assets? Be specific. Tell the stories of these men without mentioning their names.

If you stand up and think clearly and keep going for two or three minutes, that is all that will be expected of you during your first few talks. A topic, such as why you enrolled for this course, is very easy; that is obvious. If you will spend a little time selecting and arranging your material on that topic, you will be almost sure to remember it, for you will be speaking of your own observations, your own desires, your own experiences.

On the other hand, let us suppose that you have decided to speak on your business or profession. How shall you set about preparing such a talk? You already have a wealth of material on that subject. Your problem, then, will be to select and arrange it. Do not attempt to tell us all about it in three minutes. It can't be done. The attempt will be too sketchy, too fragmentary. Take one and only one phase of your topic: expand and enlarge that. For example, why not tell us how you came to be in your particular business or profession? Was it a result of accident or choice? Relate your early struggles, your defeats, your hopes, your triumphs. Give us a human interest narrative, a real-life picture based on first-hand experiences. The truthful, inside story of almost any man's life—if told modestly and without offending egotism—is most entertaining. It is almost sure-fire speech material.

Or take another angle of your business: What are its troubles? What advice would you give to a young man entering it?

Or tell us about the people with whom you come in contact—the honest and dishonest ones. Tell us of your problems with labor, your problems with your customers. What has your business taught you about the most interesting topic in the world: human nature? If you speak about the technical side of your business, about things, your talk may very easily prove uninteresting to others. But people, personalities—one can hardly go wrong with that kind of material.

Above all else, don't make your talk an abstract preachment. That will bore us. Make your talk a regular layer cake of illustrations and general statements. Think of concrete cases you have observed, and of the fundamental truths which you believe those specific instances illustrate. You will also discover that these concrete cases are far easier to remember than abstractions; they are far easier to talk about. They will also aid and brighten your delivery.

Some men, in speaking of their businesses, commit the unforgivable error of talking only of the features that interest them. Shouldn't the speaker try to ascertain what will entertain not himself but his hearers? Shouldn't he try to appeal to their selfish interests? If, for example, he sells fire insurance, shouldn't he tell them how to prevent fires on their own property? If he is a banker, shouldn't he give them advice on finance or investments?

While preparing, study your audience. Think of their wants, their wishes. That is sometimes half the battle.

In preparing some topics, it is very advisable—if time permits—to do some reading, to discover what others have thought, what others have said on the same subject. But don't read until you have first thought yourself dry. That is important—very. Then go to the public library and lay your needs before the librarian. Tell her you are preparing a speech on such and such a topic. Ask her frankly for help. If you are not in the habit of doing research work, you will probably be surprised at the aids she can put at your disposal; perhaps a special volume on your very topic, outlines and briefs for debate, giving the principal arguments on both sides of the public questions of the day, the *Reader's Guide to Periodical Literature* listing the magazine articles that have appeared on various topics since the beginning of the century, the *Daily Mail Almanac*, the Encyclopedias, and dozens of reference books. They are tools in your workshop. Use them.

THE SECRET OF RESERVE POWER

A speech ought to be prepared somewhat in a lavish and discriminating spirit. Assemble a hundred thoughts, and discard ninety.

Collect more material, more information, than there is any possibility of employing. Get it for the additional confidence it will give you, for the sureness of touch. Get it for the effect it will have on your mind and heart and whole manner of speaking. This is a basic, important factor of preparation; yet it is constantly ignored by speakers, both in public and private.

"I have drilled hundreds of salesmen, canvassers, and demonstrators," says Arthur Dunn, "and the principal weakness which I have discovered in most of them has been their failure to realize the importance of knowing everything possible about their products and getting such knowledge before they start to sell.

"Many salesmen have come to my office and after getting a description of the article and a line of sales talk have been eager to get right out and try to sell. Many of these salesmen have not lasted a week and a large number have not lasted forty-eight hours. In educating and drilling canvassers and salesmen in the sale of a food specialty, I have endeavored to make food experts of them. I have compelled them to study food charts issued by the Department of Agriculture, which show in food the amount of water, the amount of protein, the amount of carbohydrates, the amount of fat, and ash. I have had them study the elements which make up the products which they are to sell. I have had them go to school for several days and then pass examinations. I have had them sell the product to other salesmen. I have offered prizes for the best sales talks.

"I have often found salesmen who get impatient at the preliminary time required for the study of their articles. They have said, 'I will never have time to tell all of this to a retail grocer. He is too busy. If I talk protein and carbohydrates, he won't listen and, if he does listen, he won't know what I am talking about.' My reply has been, 'You don't get all of this knowledge for the benefit of your customer, but for the benefit of yourself. If you know your product from A to Z you will have a feeling about it that is difficult to describe. You will be so positively charged, so fortified, so strengthened in your own mental attitude that you will be both irresistible and unconquerable.'"

Miss Ida M. Tarbell, the well-known historian of the Standard Oil Company, told the writer that years ago, when she was in Paris, Mr. S.S. McClure, the founder of McClure's Magazine, cabled her to write a short article about the Atlantic Cable. She went to London, interviewed the European manager of the principal cable, and obtained sufficient data for her assignment. But she did not stop there. She wanted a reserve supply of facts, so she studied all manner of cables on display in the British Museum, she read books on the history of the cable and even went to manufacturing concerns on the edge of London and saw cables in the process of construction.

Why did she collect ten times as much information as she could possibly use? She did it because she felt it would give her reserve power; because she realized that the things she knew and did not express would lend force and color to the little she did express.

Edwin James Cattell has spoken to approximately thirty million people, yet he confided to me recently that if he did not, on the way home, kick himself for the good things he had left out of his talk, he felt that the performance must have been a failure. Why? Because he knew from long experience that the talks of distinct merit are those in which there abounds a reserve of material, a plethora, a profusion of it—far more than the speaker has time to use.

"What!" you object. "Does this author imagine that I can find time for all this? I would like him to know that I have a business to conduct and a wife and two children and a couple of Airedale dogs to support... I can't be running to museums and looking at cables and reading books and sitting up in bed at daylight mumbling my speeches."

My dear sir, we know all about your case, and sympathetic allowance has been made for it. The assigned topics will be questions on which you have already done considerable thinking. Sometimes you will not be asked to plan any kind of a speech in advance, but you will be given an easy topic for impromptu speaking after you face your audience. This will afford you most useful practice in thinking on your feet—the sort of thing that you may be forced to do in business discussions.

Some of the men who join this course are only slightly interested in learning to prepare talks in advance. They want to be able to think on their feet and to join in discussions that come up at various business meetings. Such students sometimes prefer to come to the class, listen, and then take their cue from some of the preceding speakers. A limited amount of this may be advisable, but don't overdo it. Follow the suggestions given in this chapter. They will give you the ease and freedom you are seeking and also the ability to prepare talks effectively.

If you procrastinate until you have leisure to prepare and plan your talk, the leisure will probably never be found. However, it is easy to do the habitual, the accustomed thing, isn't it? So why not set aside one specific evening a week, from eight to ten o'clock, to be devoted to nothing but this task? That is the sure way, the systematic way. Why not try it?

POINTS TO REMEMBER

1. Not preparing your talks can turn out to be fatal.
2. Learn how to train the mind in productivity.
3. Don't make the almost universal mistake of trying to cover too much ground in your speech.

10

VOICE CHARM

Poe said that "the tone of beauty is sadness," but he was evidently thinking from cause to effect, not contrariwise, for sadness is rarely a producer of beauty—that is peculiarly the province of joy.

The exquisite beauty of a sunset is not exhilarating but tends to a sort of melancholy that is not far from delight. The haunting beauty of deep, quiet music holds more than a tinge of sadness. The lovely minor cadences of bird song at twilight are almost depressing.

The reason we are affected to sadness by certain forms of placid beauty is twofold: Movement is stimulating and joy-producing, while quietude leads to reflection, and reflection in turn often brings out the tone of regretful longing for that which is past; secondly, quiet beauty produces a vague aspiration for the relatively unattainable, yet does not stimulate to the tremendous effort necessary to make the dimly desired state or object ours.

We must distinguish, for these reasons, between the sadness of beauty and the joy of beauty. True, joy is a deep, inner thing and takes in much more than the idea of bounding, sanguine spirits, for it includes a certain active contentedness of heart. In this chapter, however the word will have its optimistic, exuberant connotation—we are thinking now of vivid, bright-eyed, laughing joy.

Musical, joyous tones constitute voice charm, a subtle magnetism that is delightfully contagious. Now it might seem to the desultory reader that to take the lancet and cut into this alluring voice quality would be to dissect a butterfly wing and so destroy its charm. Yet how can we induce an effect if we are not certain as to the cause?

NASAL RESONANCE PRODUCES THE BELL-TONES OF THE VOICE

The tone passages of the nose must be kept entirely free for the bright tones of voice—and after our warning in the preceding chapter you will not confuse what is popularly and erroneously called a "nasal" tone with the true nasal quality, which is so well illustrated by the voice work of trained French singers and speakers.

To develop nasal resonance sing the following, dwelling as long as possible on the ng sounds. Pitch the voice in the nasal cavity. Practice both in high and low registers, and develop range—with brightness.

Sing-song. Ding-dong. Hong-kong. Long-thong.

Practice in the falsetto voice develops a bright quality in the normal speaking-voice. Try the following, and any other selections you choose, in a falsetto voice. A man's falsetto voice is extremely high and womanish, so men should not practice in falsetto after the exercise becomes tiresome.

> She perfectly scorned the best of his clan, and declared the ninth of any man, a perfectly vulgar fraction.

The actress Mary Anderson asked the poet Longfellow what she could do to improve her voice. He replied, "Read aloud daily, joyous, lyric poetry."

The joyous tones are the bright tones. Develop them by exercise. Practice your voice exercises in an attitude of joy. Under the influence of pleasure the body expands, the tone passages open, the action of heart and lungs is accelerated, and all the primary conditions for good tone are established.

More songs float out from the broken windows of the negro cabins in the South than from the palatial homes on Fifth Avenue. Henry Ward Beecher said the happiest days of his life were not when he had become an international character, but when he was an unknown minister out in Lawrenceville, Ohio, sweeping his own church, and working as a carpenter to help pay the grocer. Happiness is largely an attitude of mind, of viewing life from the right angle. The optimistic attitude can be cultivated, and it will express itself in voice charm. A telephone company recently placarded this motto in their booths: "The Voice with the Smile Wins." It does. Try it.

Reading joyous prose, or lyric poetry, will help put smile and joy of soul into your voice. The following selections are excellent for practice.

REMEMBER that when you first practice these classics you are to give sole attention to two things: a joyous attitude of heart and body, and bright tones of voice. After these ends have been attained to your satisfaction, carefully review the principles of public speaking laid down in the preceding chapters and put them into practice as you read these passages again and again. It would be better to commit each selection to memory.

In joyous conversation there is an elastic touch, a delicate stroke, upon the central ideas, generally following a pause. This elastic touch adds vivacity to the voice. If you try repeatedly, it can be sensed by feeling the tongue strike the teeth. The entire absence of elastic touch in the voice can be observed in the thick tongue of the intoxicated man. Try to talk with the tongue lying still in the bottom of the mouth, and you will obtain largely the same effect. Vivacity of utterance is gained by using the tongue to strike off the emphatic idea with a decisive, elastic touch.

Deliver the following with decisive strokes on the emphatic ideas. Deliver it in a vivacious manner, noting the elastic touch-action of the tongue. A flexible, responsive tongue is absolutely essential to good voice work.

From Napoleon's address to the directory on his return from Egypt:

> What have you done with that brilliant France which I left you? I left you at peace, and I find you at war. I left you victorious and I find you defeated. I left you the millions of Italy, and I find only spoliation and poverty. What have you done with the hundred thousand Frenchmen, my companions in glory? They are dead!... This state of affairs cannot last long; in less than three years it would plunge us into despotism.

The children at play on the street, glad from sheer physical vitality, display a resonance and charm in their voices quite different from the voices that float through the silent halls of the hospitals. A skilled physician can tell much about his patient's condition from the mere sound of the voice. Failing health, or even physical weariness, tells through the voice. It is always well to rest and be entirely refreshed before attempting to deliver a public address. As to health, neither scope nor space permits us to discuss here the laws of hygiene. There are many excellent books on this subject. In the reign of the Roman emperor Tiberius, one senator wrote to another: "To the wise, a word is sufficient."

"The apparel oft proclaims the man;" the voice always does—it is one of the greatest revealers of character. The superficial woman, the brutish man, the reprobate, the person of culture, often discloses inner nature in the voice, for even the cleverest dissembler cannot entirely prevent its tones and qualities being affected by the slightest change of thought or emotion. In anger it becomes high, harsh, and unpleasant; in love low, soft, and melodious—the variations are as limitless as they are fascinating to observe. Visit a theatrical hotel in a large city, and listen to the buzz-saw voices of the chorus girls from some burlesque "attraction." The explanation is simple—buzz-saw lives. Emerson said: "When a man lives with God his voice shall be as sweet as the murmur of the brook or the rustle of the corn." It is impossible to think selfish thoughts and have either an attractive personality, a lovely character, or a charming voice. If you want to possess voice charm, cultivate a deep, sincere sympathy for mankind. Love will shine out through your eyes and proclaim itself in your tones. One secret of the sweetness of the canary's song may be his freedom from tainted thoughts. Your character beautifies or mars your voice. As a man thinketh in his heart, so is his voice.

POINTS TO REMEMBER

1. A joyful tone of voice is charming and charismatic.
2. Develop vocal range and nasal resonance for brightness in your intonation.
3. Practice the given passage and phrases with a focus on vivacious and emphatic delivery.

11

EXPRESSING GENUINE INTEREST IN OTHERS

Expressing genuine interest in others—there's no better way to make people interested in you. People respond to people who are sincerely interested in them. They can't help but respond.

This is one of the most basic facts of human psychology. We are flattered by other people's attention. It makes us feel special. It makes us feel important. We want to be around people who show interest in us. We want to keep them close. We tend to reciprocate their interest by showing interest in them.

There are many different ways of showing interest. An expression of interest can be as simple as using a pleasant voice on the telephone. When someone calls, say hello in a tone that implies, "I'm happy to hear from you." When you see a familiar face at the shopping mall, greet the person and express a genuine pleasure at the coincidence.

Smile at people. Learn their names and how to pronounce them. Get the spellings and the titles right. Remember their birthdays. Ask about their husbands and wives and children. "I always knew that Clarence Michalis was at Bristol-Myers," says David S. Taylor, secretary-treasurer of H.G. Wellington &

Company, Inc., an investment-brokerage firm. "The minute we met, that would click. I remember those two things together. Not everybody does. I have a memory bank that would connect people with businesses."

You never know when these names will come in handy. Taylor learned this lesson when he was working as an executive in the beverage industry. "When I worked for Canada Dry," he said, "it may be hard to think why, but it was important for me to know people in the airline industry. They were a big customer. Grumman Aircraft fed a lot of people, and they had a lot of vending machines that dispensed drinks.

"It was just an entree. You could call up and say, 'Look, I'm having a problem with such-and-such.' Remembering these names and having those connections was enormously helpful."

Taylor used this technique as the basis for forming genuine relationships with people. By taking the time to remember people's names and associations, he has been able to help bring people together and solve their problems.

Don't limit those expressions of interest to the so-called important people in your life. Chances are they already get plenty of attention. Don't forget the secretaries, the assistants, the receptionists, the messengers, and all the other underrecognized people who keep your life on track. Ask about their days. It's the right thing to do—and you'll be surprised how much quicker the mail arrives at your desk in the morning.

Don't make the same mistake. When you care about someone—a friend, a spouse, a colleague—by all means let that person know. And do it while you have the chance.

Even more important than expressing interest is showing it. Harrison Conference Services, Inc., is in the business of organizing meetings and seminars, worrying about all the logistics so the clients can keep their minds focused on the real work at hand. To thrive, a company like Harrison must show its guests, over and over again, that the staff is genuinely—almost singlemindedly—interested in them.

It's not enough to have beautiful conference facilities, as Harrison certainly does. It's not enough to have attractive rooms, first-rate cuisine, high-tech audiovisual equipment, or a plethora of recreational choices, all of which Harrison has. Unless the guests feel they're being treated with genuine interest and respect, they'll take their business elsewhere.

Once you start this process, it will quickly become a natural part of your life. Before you know it, you'll be expressing interest, showing interest, and really becoming more interested in the people around you. The added benefit is that a genuine interest in others will take you outside yourself and make you less focused on whatever your own problems are.

The more you stay focused on other people, the more rewarding your personal relationships will be and the fewer negative thoughts you will have. Not a bad payback for a few kind words.

An open, friendly, interested greeting is just as important when you're the new person in the office or the new business-owner in town. The message should not be, I'm here, now what can you do for me? It should be instead, I'm here, now what can I do for you?

So volunteer at the local hospital. Sign up as a Little League coach. Join the PTA. Get involved in a local charity. These are all ways of showing interest in the community, of saying, "I care about this place." Any one of these will help you meet new people in a comfortable environment. It will be fun. It will make you feel good about yourself. It will help you develop new relationships, gain self-confidence, and it will bring you out of your comfort zone.

THERE'S NOTHING MORE EFFECTIVE AND REWARDING THAN SHOWING A GENUINE INTEREST IN OTHER PEOPLE.

> **POINTS TO REMEMBER**
>
> 1. The quickest way to make people interested in you is by showing your interest in them.
> 2. Make the effort to learn the name of the person you are interacting with; such small gestures go a long way.
> 3. Be a good listener, to be an even better speaker.

12

HOW TO CRITICIZE—AND NOT BE HATED FOR IT

Charles Schwab was passing through one of his steel mills one day at noon when he came across some of his employees smoking. Immediately above their heads was a sign that said No Smoking. Did Schwab point to the sign and say, "Can't you read?" Oh, no, not Schwab. He walked over to the men, handed each one a cigar, and said, "I'll appreciate it, boys, if you will smoke these on the outside." They knew that he knew that they had broken a rule—and they admired him because he said nothing about it and gave them a little present and made them feel important. Couldn't keep from loving a man like that, could you?

John Wanamaker used the same technique. Wanamaker used to make a tour of his great store in Philadelphia every day. Once he saw a customer waiting at a counter. No one was paying the slightest attention to her. The salespeople? Oh, they were in a huddle at the far end of the counter laughing and talking among themselves. Wanamaker didn't say a word. Quietly slipping behind the counter, he waited on the woman himself and then handed the purchase to the salespeople to be wrapped as he went on his way.

Public officials are often criticized for not being accessible to their constituents. They are busy people, and the fault sometimes lies in overprotective assistants who don't want to overburden their bosses with too many visitors. Carl Langford, who had been mayor of Orlando, Florida, the home of Disney World, for many years, frequently admonished his staff to allow people to see him. He claimed he had an "open-door" policy; yet the citizens of his community were blocked by secretaries and administrators when they called.

Finally the mayor found the solution. He removed the door from his office! His aides got the message, and the mayor had a truly open administration from the day his door was symbolically thrown away.

Simply changing one three-letter word can often spell the difference between failure and success in changing people without giving offense or arousing resentment.

Many people begin their criticism with sincere praise followed by the word "but" and ending with a critical statement. For example, in trying to change a child's careless attitude toward studies, we might say, "We're really proud of you, Johnnie, for raising your grades this term. *But* if you had worked harder on your algebra, the results would have been better."

In this case, Johnnie might feel encouraged until he heard the word "but." He might then question the sincerity of the original praise. To him, the praise might seem only to be a contrived lead-in to a critical inference of failure. Credibility would be strained, and we probably would not achieve our objective of changing Johnnie's attitude toward his studies.

This could be easily overcome by changing the word "but" to "and." "We're really proud of you, Johnnie, for raising your grades this term, *and* if you continue the same conscientious efforts next term, your algebra grade can be up with all the others."

Now, Johnnie would accept the praise because there was no follow-up of an inference of failure. We have called his attention to the behavior we wished to change indirectly, and the chances are he will try to live up to our expectations.

Calling attention indirectly to someone's mistakes works wonders with sensitive people who may resent bitterly any direct criticism. Marge Jacob of Woonsocket, Rhode Island, told one of our classes how she convinced some sloppy construction workers to clean up after themselves when they were building additions to her house.

For the first few days of the work, when Mrs. Jacob returned from her job, she noticed that the yard was strewn with the cut ends of lumber. She didn't want to antagonize the builders, because they did excellent work. So after the workers had gone home, she and her children picked up and neatly piled all the lumber debris in a corner. The following morning she called the foreman to one side and said, "I'm really pleased with the way the front lawn was left last night; it is nice and clean and does not offend the neighbors." From that day forward the workers picked up and piled the debris to one side, and the foreman came in each day seeking approval of the condition the lawn was left in after a day's work.

One of the major areas of controversy between members of the army reserves and their regular army trainers is haircuts. The reservists consider themselves civilians (which they are most of the time) and resent having to cut their hair short.

Master Sergeant Harley Kaiser of the 542nd USAR School addressed himself to this problem when he was working with a group of reserve non-commissioned officers. As an old-time regular-army master sergeant, he might have been expected to yell at his troops and threaten them. Instead he chose to make his point indirectly.

"Gentlemen," he started, "you are leaders. You will be most effective when you lead by example. You must be the example for your men to follow. You know what the army regulations say about haircuts. I am going to get my hair cut today, although it is still much shorter than some of yours. You look at yourself in the mirror, and if you feel you need a haircut to be a good example, we'll arrange time for you to visit the post barbershop."

The result was predictable. Several of the candidates did look in the mirror and went to the barbershop that afternoon and received "regulation" haircuts. Sergeant Kaiser commented the next morning that he already could see the development of leadership qualities in some of the members of the squad.

On March 8, 1887, the eloquent Henry Ward Beecher died. The following Sunday, Lyman Abbott was invited to speak in the pulpit left silent by Beecher's passing. Eager to do his best, he wrote, rewrote, and polished his sermon with the meticulous care of a Flaubert. Then he read it to his wife. It was poor—as most written speeches are. She might have said, if she had had less judgment, "Lyman, that is terrible. That'll never do. You'll put people to sleep. It reads like an encyclopedia. You ought to know better than that after all the years you have been preaching. For heaven's sake, why don't you talk like a human being? Why don't you act natural? You'll disgrace yourself if you ever read that stuff."

That's what she *might* have said. And, if she had, you know what would have happened. And she knew too. So, she merely remarked that it would make an excellent article for the *North American Review*. In other words, she praised it and at the same time subtly suggested that it wouldn't do as a speech. Lyman Abbott saw the point, tore up his carefully prepared manuscript, and preached without even using notes.

POINTS TO REMEMBER

1. Modify your vocabulary to soften the blow of criticism.
2. Never directly address someone's error.
3. If you have to criticize once, praise thrice.

13

MAKING PEOPLE GLAD TO DO WHAT YOU WANT

Back in 1915, America was aghast. For more than a year, the nations of Europe had been slaughtering one another on a scale never before dreamed of in all the bloody annals of mankind. Could peace be brought about? No one knew. But Woodrow Wilson was determined to try. He would send a personal representative, a peace emissary, to counsel with the warlords of Europe.

William Jennings Bryan, secretary of state, Bryan, the peace advocate, longed to go. He saw a chance to perform a great service and make his name immortal. But Wilson appointed another man, his intimate friend and adviser Colonel Edward M. House; and it was House's thorny task to break the unwelcome news to Bryan without giving him offence.

"Bryan was distinctly disappointed when he heard I was to go to Europe as the peace emissary," Colonel House records in his diary. "He said he had planned to do this himself...

"I replied that the President thought it would be unwise for anyone to do this officially, and *that his going would attract a great deal of attention* and people would wonder why he was there..."

You see the intimation? House practically told Bryan that he was *too important* for the job—and Bryan was satisfied.

Colonel House, adroit, experienced in the ways of the world, was following one of the important rules of human relations: *Always make the other person happy about doing the thing you suggest.*

Woodrow Wilson followed that policy even when inviting William Gibbs McAdoo to become a member of his cabinet. That was the highest honor he could confer upon anyone, and yet Wilson extended the invitation in such a way as to make McAdoo feel doubly important. Here is the story in McAdoo's own words: "He [Wilson] said that he was making up his cabinet and that he would be very glad if I would accept a place in it as Secretary of the Treasury. He had a delightful way of putting things; he created the impression that by accepting this great honor I would be doing him a favor."

Unfortunately, Wilson didn't always employ such tact. If he had, history might have been different. For example, Wilson didn't make the Senate and the Republican Party happy by entering the United States in the League of Nations. Wilson refused to take such prominent Republican leaders as Elihu Root or Charles Evans Hughes or Henry Cabot Lodge to the peace conference with him. Instead, he took along unknown men from his own party. He snubbed the Republicans, refused to let them feel that the League was their idea as well as his, refused to let them have a finger in the pie; and, as a result of this crude handling of human relations, wrecked his own career, ruined his health, shortened his life, caused America to stay out of the League and altered the history of the world.

Statesmen and diplomats aren't the only ones who use this make-a-person-happy-to-do-things-you-want-them-to-do-approach. Dale O. Ferrier of Fort Wayne, Indiana, told how he encouraged one of his young children to willingly do the chore he was assigned.

"One of Jeff's chores was to pick up pears from under the pear tree so the person who was mowing underneath wouldn't have to stop to pick them up. He didn't like this chore, and frequently it was either not done at all or it was done so poorly that the mower had to stop and pick up several pears that he had missed. Rather than have an eyeball-to-eyeball confrontation about it, one day I said to him: 'Jeff, I'll make a deal with you. For every bushel basket full of pears you pick up, I'll pay you one dollar. But after you are finished, for every pear I find left in the yard, I'll take away a dollar. How does that sound?' As you would expect, he not only picked up all of the pears, but I had to keep an eye on him to see that he didn't pull a few off the trees to fill up some of the baskets."

I knew a man who had to refuse many invitations to speak, invitations extended by friends, invitations coming from people to whom he was obligated; and yet he did it so adroitly that the other person was at least contented with his refusal. How did he do it? Not by merely talking about the fact that he was too busy and too-this and too-that. No, after expressing his appreciation of the invitation and regretting his inability to accept it, he suggested a substitute speaker. In other words, he didn't give the other person any time to feel unhappy about the refusal. He immediately changed the other person's thoughts to some other speaker who could accept the invitation.

Gunter Schmidt, who took our course in West Germany, told of an employee in the food store he managed who was negligent about putting the proper price tags on the shelves where the items were displayed. This caused confusion and customer complaints. Reminders, admonitions, confrontations with her about this did not do much good. Finally, Mr. Schmidt called her into his office and told her he was appointing her Supervisor of Price Tag Posting for the entire store and she would be responsible for keeping all of the shelves properly tagged. This new responsibility and title changed her attitude completely, and she fulfilled her duties satisfactorily from then on.

Childish? Perhaps. But that is what they said to Napoleon when he created the Legion of Honour and distributed 15,000 crosses to his soldiers and made eighteen of his generals "Marshals of France" and called his troops the "Grand Army". Napoleon was criticized for giving "toys" to war-hardened veterans, and Napoleon replied, "Men are ruled by toys."

This technique of giving titles and authority worked for Napoleon and it will work for you. For example, a friend of mine, Mrs Ernest Gent of Scarsdale, New York, was troubled by boys running across and destroying her lawn. She tried coaxing. Neither worked. Then she tried giving the worst sinner in the gang a title and a feeling of authority. She made him her "detective" and put him in charge of keeping all trespassers off her lawn. That solved her problem. Her "detective" built a bonfire in the backyard, heated an iron red hot and threatened to brand any boy who stepped on the lawn.

The effective leader should keep the following guidelines in mind when it is necessary to change attitudes or behaviour:

1. Be sincere. Do not promise anything that you cannot deliver. Forget about the benefits to yourself and concentrate on the benefits to the other person.
2. Know exactly what it is you want the other person to do.
3. Be empathetic. Ask yourself what is it the other person really wants.

4. Consider the benefits that person will receive from doing what you suggest.
5. Match those benefits to the other person's wants.
6. When you make your request, put it in a form that will convey to the other person the idea that he personally will benefit. We could give a curt order like this: "John, we have customers coming in tomorrow and I need the stockroom cleaned out. So sweep it out, put the stock in neat piles on the shelves and polish the counter." Or we could express the same idea by showing John the benefits he will get from doing the task: "John, we have a job that should be completed right away. If it is done now, we won't be faced with it later. I am bringing some customers in tomorrow to show our facilities. I would like to show them the stockroom, but it is in poor shape. If you could sweep it out, put the stock in neat piles on the shelves and polish the counter, it would make us look efficient and you will have done your part to provide a good company image."

Will John be happy about doing what you suggest? Probably not very happy, but happier than if you had not pointed out the benefits. Assuming you know that John has pride in the way stockroom looks and is interested in contributing to the company image, he will be more likely to be cooperative. It also will have been pointed out to John that the job would have to be done eventually and by doing it now, he won't be faced with it later.

It is naïve to believe you will always get a favourable reaction from other persons when you use these approaches, but the experience of most people shows that you are more likely to change attitudes this way than by not using these principles—and if you increase your success by even a mere 10 per cent, you have become 10 per cent more effective as a leader than you were before—and that is *your* benefit.

> **POINTS TO REMEMBER**
> 1. Always make the other person happy about doing the thing you suggest.
> 2. If you have to refuse someone, do it nicely!
> 3. The guidelines to follow to become an effective leader.

14

THE TALK TO CONVINCE

Quintilian described the orator as "a good man skilled in speaking." He was talking about sincerity and character. Nothing said in this book, nor anything which will be said, can take the place of this essential attribute of speaking effectiveness. Pierpont Morgan said that character was the best way to obtain credit; it is also the best way to win the confidence of the audience.

"The sincerity with which a man speaks," said Alexander Woolcott, "imparts to his voice a color of truth no perjurer can feign."

Especially when the purpose of our talk is to convince, it is necessary to set forth our own ideas with the inner glow that comes from sincere conviction. We must first be convinced before we attempt to convince others.

SPEAK WITH CONTAGIOUS ENTHUSIASM

Contradicting ideas are much less likely to arise in the listener's mind when the speaker presents his ideas with feeling and contagious enthusiasm. I say "contagious," for enthusiasm is just that. It thrusts aside all negative and opposing ideas. When your aim is to convince, remember it is more productive to stir emotions than to arouse thoughts. Feelings are more powerful than cold ideas. To arouse feelings one must be intensely in earnest. Regardless of the petty phrases a man may concoct, regardless of the illustrations he may assemble, regardless of the harmony of his voice and the grace of his gestures, if he does not speak sincerely, these are hollow and glittering trappings. If you would impress an audience, be impressed yourself. Your spirit, shining through your eyes, radiating through your voice, and proclaiming itself through your manner, will communicate itself to your audience.

Every time you speak, and especially when your avowed purpose is to convince, what you do determines the attitude of your listeners. If you are lukewarm, so will they be; if you are flippant and antagonistic, so will they be. "When the congregation falls asleep," wrote Henry Ward Beecher, "there is only one thing to do; provide the usher with a sharp stick and have him prod the preacher."

I was once one of three judges called on to award the Curtis medal at Columbia University. There were half a dozen undergraduates, all of them elaborately trained, all of them eager to acquit themselves well. But—with only a single exception— what they were striving for was to win the medal. They had little or no desire to convince.

They had chosen their topics because these topics permitted oratorical development. They had no deep personal interest in the arguments they were making. And their successive talks were merely exercises in the art of delivery.

The exception was a Zulu Prince. He had selected as his theme "The Contribution of Africa to Modern Civilization." He put intense feeling into every word he uttered. His talk was no mere exercise; it was a living thing, born of conviction and enthusiasm. He spoke as the representative of his people, of his continent; with wisdom, high character, and good will, he brought us a message of his people's hopes and a plea for our understanding.

We gave him the medal although he was possibly no more accomplished in addressing a large group than two or three of his competitors. What we judges recognized was that his talk had the true fire of sincerity; it was ablaze with truth. Beside it, the other talks were only flickering gas-logs.

The Prince had learned in his own way in a distant land that you can't project your personality in a talk to others by using reason alone: you have to reveal to them how deeply you yourself believe in what you say.

SHOW RESPECT AND AFFECTION FOR YOUR AUDIENCE

"The human personality demands love and it also demands respect," Dr. Norman Vincent Peale said as a prelude to speaking of a professional comedian. "Every human being has an inner sense of worth, of importance, of dignity. Wound that and you have lost that person forever. So when you love and respect a person you build him up and, accordingly, he loves and esteems you.

"At one time I was on a program with an entertainer. I did not know the man well, but since that meeting I read that he was having difficulty, and I think I know why.

"I had been sitting beside him quietly for I was about to speak. 'You aren't nervous, are you?' he asked

"'Why, yes,' I replied. 'I always get a little nervous before I stand up before an audience. I have a profound respect for an audience and the responsibility makes me a bit nervous. Don't you get nervous?'

"'No,' he said, 'Why should I? Audiences fall for anything. They are a lot of dopes.'

"'I don't agree with you,' I said. They are your sovereign judges. I have great respect for audiences.'"

When he read about this man's waning popularity Dr. Peale was sure the reason lay in an attitude that antagonized others instead of winning them.

What an object lesson for all of us who want to impart something to other people!

BEGIN IN A FRIENDLY WAY

An atheist once challenged William Paley to disprove his contention that there was no Supreme Being. Very quietly Paley took out his watch, opened the case, and said: "If I were to tell you that those levers and wheels and springs made themselves and fitted themselves together and started running on their own account, wouldn't you question my intelligence? Of course, you would. But look up at the stars. Every one of them has its perfect appointed course and motion—the earth and planets around the sun, and the whole group pitching along at more than a million miles a day. Each star is another sun with its own group of worlds, rushing on through space like our own solar system. Yet there are no collisions, no disturbance, no confusion. All quiet, efficient, and controlled. Is it easier to believe that they just happened or that someone made them so?"

Suppose he had retorted to his antagonist at the outset: "No God? Don't be a silly ass. You don't know what you are talking about." What would have happened? Doubtlessly a verbal joust—a wordy war would have ensued, as futile as it was fiery. The atheist would have risen with an unholy zeal upon him to fight for his opinions with all the fury of a wildcat.

Why? Because, as Professor Overstreet has pointed out, they were *his* opinions, and his precious, indispensable self-esteem would have been threatened; his pride would have been at stake.

Since pride is such a fundamentally explosive characteristic of human nature, wouldn't it be the part of wisdom to get a man's pride working for us, instead of against us? How? By showing, as Paley did, that the thing we propose is very similar to something that our opponent already believes. That renders it easier for him to accept than to reject your proposal. That prevents contradictory and opposing ideas from arising in the mind to vitiate what we have said.

Paley showed delicate appreciation of how the human mind functions. Most men, however, lack this subtle ability to enter the citadel of a man's beliefs arm in arm with the owner. They erroneously imagine that in order to take the citadel, they must storm it, batter it down by a frontal attack. What happens? The moment hostilities commence, the drawbridge is lifted, the great gates are slammed and bolted, the mailed archers draw their long bows—the battle of words and wounds is on. Such frays always end in a draw; neither has convinced the other of anything.

This more sensible method I am advocating is not new. It was used long ago by Saint Paul. He employed it in that famous address of his to the Athenians on Mars Hill—employed it with an adroitness and finesse that compels our admiration across nineteen centuries. He was a man of finished education; and, after his conversion to Christianity, his eloquence made him its leading advocate. One day he arrived at Athens—the post-Pericles Athens, an Athens that had passed the summit of its glory and was now on the decline. The Bible says of it at this period: "All the Athenians and strangers which were there spent their time in nothing else but either to tell or to hear some new thing."

No radios, no cables, no news dispatches; those Athenians must have been hard put in those days to scratch up something fresh every afternoon. Then Paul came. Here was something new. They crowded about him, amused, curious, interested. Taking him to the Aeropagus, they said: "May we know what this new doctrine, whereof thou speakest, is? For thou bringest certain strange things to our ears: we would know therefore what these things mean."

In other words, they invited a speech; and, nothing loath, Paul agreed. In fact, that was what he had come for. He probably stood up on a block or stone, and, being a bit nervous, as all good speakers are at the very outset, he may have given his hands a dry wash, and have cleared his throat before he began.

However, he did not altogether approve of the way they had worded their invitation; "New doctrines…strange things." That was poison. He must eradicate those ideas. They were fertile ground for the propagating of contradictory and clashing opinions. He did not wish to present his faith as something strange and alien. He wanted to tie it up to, liken it to, something they already believed. That would smother dissenting suggestions. But how? He thought a moment; hit upon a brilliant plan; he began his immortal address: "Ye men of Athens, I perceive that in all things ye are very superstitious."

Some translations read, "Ye are very religious." I think that is better, more accurate. They worshipped many gods; they were very religious. They were proud of it. He complimented them, pleased them. They began to warm toward him. One of the rules of the art of effective speaking is to support a statement by an illustration. He does just that:

"For, as I passed by, and beheld your devotions, I found an altar with this inscription, TO THE UNKNOWN GOD."

That proves, you see, that they were very religious. They were so afraid of slighting one of the deities that they had put up an altar to the unknown God, a sort of blanket insurance policy to provide against all unconscious slights and unintentional oversights. Paul, by mentioning this specific altar, indicated that he was not dealing in flattery; he showed that his remark was a genuine appreciation born of observation.

Now, here comes the consummate rightness of this opening: "Whom therefore ye ignorantly worship, Him declare I unto you."

"New doctrine...strange things?" Not a bit of it. He was there merely to explain a few truths about a God they were already worshipping without being conscious of it. Likening the things they did not believe, you see, to something they already passionately accepted—such was his superb technique.

He pronounced his doctrine of salvation and resurrection, quoted a few words from one of their own Greek poets; and he was done. Some of his hearers mocked, but others said, "We will hear thee again on this matter."

Our problem in making a talk to convince or impress others is just this: to plant the idea in their minds and to keep contradicting and opposing ideas from arising. He who is skilled in doing that has power in speaking and influencing others. Here is precisely where the rules in my book *How to Win Friends and Influence People* will be helpful.

Almost every day of your life you are talking to people who differ from you on some subject under discussion. Aren't you constantly trying to win people to your way of thinking, at home, in the office, in social situations of all kinds? Is there room for improvement in your methods? How do you begin? By showing Lincoln's tact and Macmillan's? If so, you are a person of rare diplomacy and extraordinary discretion. It is well to remember Woodrow Wilson's words, "If you come to me and say, 'Let us sit down and take counsel together, and, if we differ from one another, understand why it is that we differ from one another, just what the points at issue are,' we will presently find that we are not so far apart after all, that the points on which we differ are few and the points on which we agree are many, and that if we only have the patience and the candor and the desire to get together, we will get together."

POINTS TO REMEMBER
1. The speech should reflect your sincerity.
2. Benefit from the 'Yes-Response' technique.
3. Friendly approach with the audience enables them to connect with you better.

15

NO ONE LIKES TO TAKE ORDERS

I once had the pleasure of dining with Mrs. Ida Tarbell, the dean of American biographers. When I told her I was writing this book, we began discussing this all-important subject of getting along with people, and she told me that while she was writing her biography of Owen D. Young, she interviewed a man who had sat for three years in the same office with Mr. Young. This man declared that during all that time he had never heard Owen D. Young give a direct order to anyone. He always gave suggestions, not orders. Owen D. Young never said, for example, "Do this or do that," or "Don't do this or don't do that." He would say, "You might consider this," or "Do you think that would work?" Frequently he would say, after he had dictated a letter, "What do you think of this?" In looking over a letter of one of his assistants, he would say, "Maybe if we were to phrase it this way it would be better." He always gave people the opportunity to do things themselves; he never told his assistants to do things; he let them do them, let them learn from their mistakes.

A technique like that makes it easy for a person to correct errors. A technique like that saves a person's pride and gives him or her a feeling of importance. It encourages cooperation instead of rebellion.

Resentment caused by a brash order may last a long time—even if the order was given to correct an obviously bad situation. Dan Santarelli, a teacher at a vocational school in Wyoming, Pennsylvania, told one of our classes how one of his students had blocked the entranceway to one of the school's shops by illegally parking his car in it. One of the other instructors stormed into the classroom and asked in an arrogant tone, "Whose car is blocking the driveway?" When the student who owned the car responded, the instructor screamed: "Move that car and move it right now, or I'll wrap a chain around it and drag it out of there."

Now that student was wrong. The car should not have been parked there. But from that day on, not only did that student resent the instructor's action, but all the students in the class did everything they could to give the instructor a hard time and make his job unpleasant.

How could he have handled it differently? If he had asked in a friendly way, "Whose car is in the driveway?" and then suggested that if it were moved, other cars could get in and out, the student would have gladly moved it and neither he nor his classmates would have been upset and resentful.

Asking questions not only makes an order more palatable; it often stimulates the creativity of the persons whom you ask. People are more likely to accept an order if they have had a part in the decision that caused the order to be issued.

When Ian Macdonald of Johannesburg, South Africa, the general manager of a small manufacturing plant specializing in precision machine parts, had the opportunity to accept a very large order, he was convinced that he would not meet the promised delivery date. The work already scheduled in the shop and the short completion time needed for this order made it seem impossible for him to accept the order.

Instead of pushing his people to accelerate their work and rush the order through, he called everybody together, explained the situation to them, and told them how much it would mean to the company and to them if they could make it possible to produce the order on time. Then he started asking questions:

"Is there anything we can do to handle this order?"

"Can anyone think of different ways to process it through the shop that will make it possible to take the order?"

"Is there any way to adjust our hours or personnel assignments that would help?"

The employees came up with many ideas and insisted that he take the order. They approached it with a "We can do it" attitude, and the order was accepted, produced, and delivered on time.

POINTS TO REMEMBER

1. Not necessary to directly call out someone on their mistake.
2. Leave the accusatory tone and opt for a friendly one.
3. Create a safe space for everyone around you so they can come to you with problems.

16

CAPTURING YOUR AUDIENCE AT ONCE

Shortly after the close of World War I, the late Senator Lodge and President Lowell of Harvard were scheduled to debate the League of Nations question before a Boston audience. Senator Lodge felt that most of the audience were hostile to his view; yet he must win them to his way of thinking. How? By a direct, frontal, aggressive attack on their convictions? Ah, no. The Senator was far too shrewd a psychologist to bungle his plea with such crude tactics. He began with supreme tact, with admirable finesse. The opening of his speech is quoted in the following paragraph. Note that even his most bitter opponents could not have differed with the sentiments expressed in his first dozen sentences. Note how he appeals to their emotion of patriotism in his salutation: "My Fellow Americans." Observe how he minimizes the differences in the views they are to defend, and how he deftly stresses the things they cherish in common.

See how he praises his opponent, how he insists upon the fact that they differ only on minor details of method, and not at all upon the vital question of the welfare of America and the peace of the world. He even goes further and admits that he is in favor of a League of Nations of some kind. So, in the last analysis, he differed from his opponent only in this: he felt that we ought to have a more ideal and efficacious League.

Your Excellency, Ladies and Gentlemen, My Fellow Americans:

I am largely indebted to President Lowell for this opportunity to address this great audience. He and I are friends of many years, both Republicans. He is the president of our great university, one of the most important and influential places in the United States. He is also an eminent student and historian of politics and government. He and I may differ as to methods in this great question now before the people, but I am sure that in regard to the security of the peace of the world and the welfare of the United States we do not differ in purposes.

"I am going to say a single word, if you will permit me, as to my own position. I have tried to state it over and over again. I thought I had stated it in plain English. But there are those who find in misrepresentation a convenient weapon for controversy, and there are others, most excellent people, who perhaps have not seen what I have said and who possibly have misunderstood me. It has been said that I am against any League of Nations. I am not; far from it. I am anxious to have the nations, the free nations of the world, united in a league, as we call it, a society, as the French call it, but united, to do all that can be done to secure the future peace of the world and to bring about a general disarmament.

No matter how determined you were beforehand to differ with a speaker, an opening like that would make you soften and relent a bit, wouldn't it? Wouldn't it make you willing to listen to more? Wouldn't it tend to convince you of the speaker's fairmindedness?

What would have been the result had Senator Lodge set out immediately to show those who believed in the League of Nations that they were hopelessly in error, cherishing a delusion? The result would have been futile; the following quotation from Professor James Harvey Robinson's enlightening and popular book *The Mind in the Making* shows the psychological reason why such an attack would have been futile:

> We sometimes find ourselves changing our minds without any resistance or heavy emotion, but if we are told we are wrong we resent the imputation and harden our hearts. We are incredibly heedless in the formation of our beliefs, but find ourselves filled with an illicit passion for them when anyone proposes to rob us of their companionship. It is obviously not the ideas themselves that are dear to us, but our self-esteem which is threatened... The little word *my* is the most important one in human affairs, and properly to reckon with it is the beginning of wisdom. It has the same force whether it is *my* dinner, *my* dog and *my* house, or *my* faith, *my* country and *my* God. We not only resent the imputation that our watch is wrong, or our car shabby, but that our conception of the canals of Mars, of the pronunciation of 'Epictetus', of the medicinal value of salicine, or of the date of Sargon I, are subject to revision.... We like to continue to believe what we have been accustomed to accept as true, and the resentment aroused when doubt is cast upon any of our assumptions leads us to seek every manner of excuse for clinging to it. The result is that most of our so-called reasoning consists in finding arguments for going on believing as we already do.

THE BEST ARGUMENT IS AN EXPLANATION

Is it not quite evident that the speaker who argues with his audience is merely arousing their stubbornness, putting them on the defensive, making it well nigh impossible for them to change their minds? Is it wise to start by saying, "I am going to prove so and so?" Aren't your hearers liable to accept that as a challenge and remark silently, "Let's see you do it."

Is it not much more advantageous to begin by stressing something that you and all of your hearers believe, and then to raise some pertinent question that everyone would like to have answered? Then take your audience with you in an earnest search for the answer. While on that search, present the facts as you see them so clearly that they will unconsciously be led to accept your conclusions as their own. They will have much more faith in some truth that they believe they have discovered for themselves. "The best argument is that which seems merely an explanation."

In every controversy, no matter how wide and bitter the differences, there is always some common ground of agreement on which the speaker can invite everyone to assemble for the search after facts that he is going to conduct. To illustrate: even if the head of the Communist Party were addressing a convention of the Bankers' Association, he could find some mutual beliefs, some analogous desires to share with his hearers. Couldn't he? Let us see:

> Poverty has always been one of the cruel problems of human society. We have always felt it our duty to alleviate, whenever and wherever possible, the sufferings of the poor. We are a generous nation. No other people in all history have poured out their wealth so prodigally,

so unselfishly to help the unfortunate. Now, with this same mental generosity and spiritual unselfishness that has characterized our givings in the past, let us examine together the facts of our industrial life and see if we can find some means, fair and just and acceptable to all, that will tend to prevent as well as to mitigate the evils of poverty.

Who could object to that? Could Father Coughlin, or Norman Thomas, or J. Pierpont Morgan? Hardly.

Do we seem to be contradicting here the gospel of force and energy and enthusiasm? Hardly. There is a time for everything. But the time for force is seldom in the beginning of a talk. Tact is more likely to be needed then.

POINTS TO REMEMBER

1. Avoid taking an aggressive approach with the audience.
2. Appeal to the emotion and thought of the crowd that is mutual to most.
3. It is not what you say but how you say it that separates a good speaker from a bad one.